M000023220

how to use the
healing
power
of your
planets

how to use the
healing
power
of your
planets

induce better health
and well-being

donna taylor

quantum

LONDON • NEW YORK • TORONTO • SYDNEY

quantum

An imprint of W. Foulsham & Co. Ltd
The Publishing House, Bennetts Close, Cippenham, Slough,
Berkshire, SL1 5AP, England

ISBN 0-572-02855-5

Copyright © 2003 Donna Taylor

Cover illustration by Jurgen Ziewe

All rights reserved.

The moral right of the author has been asserted.

The Copyright Act prohibits (subject to certain very
limited exceptions) the making of copies of any
copyright work or of a substantial part of such a work,
including the making of copies by photocopying or
similar process. Written permission to make a copy or
copies must therefore normally be obtained from the
publisher in advance. It is advisable also to consult the
publisher if in any doubt as to the legality of any copying
which is to be undertaken.

The suggestions for remedies in this book are intended as general guidelines
only. If you are considering using aromatherapy oils, taking herbs or
supplementing your diet with vitamins and minerals, please consult a
qualified practitioner beforehand. Many herbs are unsafe taken in large
quantities or by certain people with certain conditions, and various
aromatherapy oils are toxic and are harmful during pregnancy. It is beyond
the scope of this book to list all the possible dangers present with these
therapies, so always consult a qualified practitioner before self-prescription.

Neither the editors of W. Foulsham & Co. Ltd nor the author nor the
publisher take responsibility for any possible consequences from any
treatment, procedure, test, exercise, action or application of medication or
preparation by any person reading or following the information in this
book. The publication of this book does not constitute the practice of
medicine, and this book does not attempt to replace any diet or instructions
from your doctor. The author and publisher advise the reader to check with
a doctor before administering any medication or undertaking any course of
treatment or exercise.

Printed in Great Britain by St Edmundsbury Press, Bury St Edmunds, Suffolk

Contents

Acknowledgements

The road to becoming a professional astrologer isn't always an easy one and this book would never have materialised were it not for the help, support and belief of many people.

Perhaps most deserving of my gratitude are my students and clients – past and present – for it is they who believe in me enough to part with their hard-earned cash and inspire me with their enthusiastic feedback. Thank you all – especially to the three clients who generously offered themselves for examination in the case studies.

My gratitude also goes out to all those who have offered me opportunities to progress this far: Jill Keene at Natural Health and Well-being, without whom this book would probably still be just a vague notion languishing in the depths of my subconscious; my publisher Wendy Hobson, for seeing the potential in this work and guiding me accordingly; Alex Hall, Sandra Goodman, Stephen Firth, Kit Sadgrove, Pamela Nancarrow and Avril Quincey.

Deep appreciation to all those who encouraged me when the going got tough and refrained from telling me to 'get a proper job', in particular Michael Korendowych – where are you?

A big thank you to the creative members of the team: Andy Campbell for artistic skills right from the very beginning and Steve Johnson for all his design work over the last few years. Much gratitude also to Ian Ingram for his painstaking efforts with the jacket photograph and for not laughing all those years ago at art college when I wanted to photograph zodiac signs! So glad our paths have crossed again.

Technology has never been my strong point, so thank you to Richard Schofield and David Jessop for bailing me out at the last minute.

Special thanks to my parents for their long-suffering material support and to Tony for love, tenderness and belief, not to mention his illustrations and diligent reading of first proofs with thoughtful suggestions for improvements.

And finally, a huge thank you to Trevor Morris, who played such an instrumental part in shaping me into the astrologer who finally sat down to write this book. The journey was not always a comfortable one, but without you I probably wouldn't be where I am today.

Foreword

This book was born from a combination of factors – a love of astrology, a passion for health and a desire for people to achieve their potential and follow their dreams. I have felt an affinity with astrology for as long as I can remember and developed an interest in health and alternative therapies in my teens. Wanting people to be happy and fulfilled came later, when I realised how glorious life can be when we follow our hearts.

I soon realised that astrology can offer us the key to unlocking the heart and directing us towards the path that we always wanted to tread before we got lost and meandered off in some other direction. I also realised that astrology can stand alone in its power as a diagnostic tool, because it can help us to achieve wholeness, which is after all where good health stems from. By understanding our natal astrological chart, we can start to understand who we really are and what we really need. This in turn allows for a more balanced and harmonious state of being.

With these realisations, I decided to create a self-help book through which people could not only begin to understand themselves better but also learn to see how strongly their health is connected to their ability to express themselves and live a fulfilling life.

So, although this book may be described as a book about astrology and health, it's actually a book about following your heart and being the person you were always meant to be. Because, quite simply, there is no better way of achieving health and well-being.

Introduction

*'The world is not in need of a new religion, nor is
the world in need of a new philosophy: what the
world needs is healing and regeneration.'*
JOEL S. GOLDSMITH, *The Art of Spiritual Healing*

For anyone involved in healing, this is an exciting time to be alive. We have never had so many natural therapies to choose from and some of them, such as aromatherapy, acupuncture and reflexology, are now much more readily available and are recognised by the medical establishment – progress indeed. Perhaps most exciting of all, though, is the new awareness gradually seeping into people's consciousness that illness is a reflection of something deeper. An attack of ME or a heart in need of attention is no longer always merely dismissed as a failing body completely disconnected from us. We are beginning to recognise that such problems are symptomatic of a lack of fulfilment in some area. They are a physical reflection that something somewhere in our lives isn't working. We can read about this growing awareness in best-selling metaphysical books by Louise Hay, Gill Edwards, Caroline Myss, Debbie Shapiro and others who tell how symptoms are metaphors for faulty thought patterns or negative emotions. The wonderful thing about all this is that we're starting to take more responsibility for our lives as we realise that illness isn't something that happens to us; illness is something we create.

However, the vast range of therapies now available have a little catching up to do – and this includes astrology. Every therapist needs to be aware that clients with chronic ailments have something else going on – something in their lives that they're not happy about, or an aspect of themselves that they're not fulfilling. Treating them physically isn't always enough. What's often needed is change, and as therapists we need to be able to recognise when a person is in need of change and to be able to support and guide him or her through it.

As we shall see, astrology stands alone in its ability to help facilitate this change, which may come as a surprise to many people whose knowledge of astrology extends only to their Sun sign. When we gaze up at the stars, few of us would ever think that the planets could have an effect on our health, and yet Culpeper, the famous herbalist, said long ago, 'medicine without astrology is like a lamp without oil'. Hippocrates also pronounced that 'a physician without a knowledge of astrology had better call himself a fool rather than a physician'. Certainly, as a healing tool, astrology is like no other in that it is capable – like a metaphysical x-ray – of identifying all the potential problems that we carry around and what we need for healing.

The astrological birth chart is a mirror of the soul. Reflected in your chart is every iota of talent, every ability, every need and desire. In this mirror image we can also see every wrinkle of discontent, every sagging of fear and every line of insecurity. Childhood themes can be identified, giving us an idea of how the individual's beliefs and attitudes have been formed, what negative patterns might have emerged as a result of the imperfect childhood that we all experience, and the physical weaknesses that we may display as a result of these themes, beliefs and attitudes. Our astrological chart, then, displays the reflection that can empower us to change our lives, if we just have the courage to use it.

In this book, I have tried to break new ground by identifying what lies at the heart of the possible difficulties contained within our planetary combinations and how to redress any imbalances. Used correctly, this book should be able to help you shed new light upon your physical and emotional weaknesses and what your symptoms are trying to tell you. If there's one thing I've learned as an astrological counsellor and healer, it's that illness is a call for change, and change requires courage. So at the end of the day, your potential for health and happiness lies in your hands and in your ability to believe in yourself enough to make the changes you need.

How to use this book

This book was created so that people may understand themselves and the reasons for their symptoms better so that they can lead happier, healthier, more fulfilling lives. A thorough knowledge of astrology is by no means essential to achieve this state of well-being, because you will become aware quite quickly where you are out of balance simply by reading about each of the planets. The suggestions for creating balance, if heeded, will help you to create better health and facilitate a sense of wholeness.

To use the information to the full, you will need your natal chart. Ideally, having your own natal chart drawn up and interpreted will enable you to gain the most accurate picture of your inner self, and how that then manifests on an outer level through your health. If you don't already have a print-out of your natal chart, there are several ways in which you can get one done.

○ Contact a professional astrologer who will draw up your chart and explain it to you (see page 180).

○ Follow the avenues that offer free charts. Someone you know with an astrological computer program might be happy to print off your chart. Some programs even include interpretations and, though these are likely to be basic, you will at least be presented with a list of all your planetary positions and aspects. Alternatively, there are numerous internet astrology sites that allow you to print out your chart for free (see page 180). If you don't have access to the internet at home, you can usually get online at your local library.

○ If you wish to go deeper, you could draw up your own chart or work out your planetary positions and aspects from astronomical data. This is a more complex route and one that we can only touch on in a book of this kind, but I have provided a basic step-by-step guide on pages 164–170.

So, now that you have no excuse for not having a copy of your chart sitting in front of you while you read this book, let's look at how you can get the most out of the information contained within.

The role of the planets

I have tried to capture the essence of each planet and stress how important it is that we live in harmony with the energy of this planet. It may help to think of the planets as living beings, or personalities. Mars, for example, has a warring, courageous and impetuous personality. However, the sign, position and aspects of Mars in your chart will colour its personality, and a Mars in Capricorn, or inhibited by Saturn, will need to be expressed somewhat differently to someone who has Mars located in Aries or amplified by the Sun. This is why it's so important to understand what the unique combinations of planets in your chart need in order to keep them (and you) happy and healthy. As children and teenagers we do this naturally, but as we get older it becomes all too easy to neglect parts of ourselves that used to be easily expressed. We become slowly detached from the person we used to be, through a mix of reserve, fear, daily pressures and negative beliefs. As you get to understand yourself better through your birth chart, you will become aware which planets and areas you are neglecting and how this may be making you discontent.

Obviously some people may have a particular planet pronounced in their chart and so they are unlikely to have a problem expressing that personality, or in some cases they might overdo the energy of that planet. To have some planets more dominant than others is okay – we are all here to learn different things and the vastly differing natures of the planets allow us to experience these differences to greater or lesser extents. But the important thing to avoid is the denial or suppression of parts of ourselves, which can happen all too easily if we're not vigilant. Another possible difficulty occurs when we over-identify with one particular planet, which not only makes for an imbalanced personality but also leaves us in a weak and vulnerable state when a planetary transit of an opposite nature occurs.

So take on board the requirements of each planet. The key is to neither overdo nor underdo.

Remedies

The selection of remedies chosen to counteract the difficult energies between the planets are those that I feel would work well in chart analysis: aromatherapy oils, Bach flower remedies, herbs, colours, and vitamins and minerals. In some cases, a philosophy is more relevant, and for very troublesome energies I have selected the particular therapy that I feel would have the best results.

Each remedy has been selected with a view to working in harmony with the problem, or compensating for a lack. The colours that I have chosen are not the colours normally associated with the planets in question. For example, Mars's colour is red, but if someone's chart has a lot of fire or Mars aspects, or if he or she is suffering from anger, aggression, irritation or impatience, red would perhaps not be the best colour to be surrounded by. Soothing pastels and tranquil greens would have a far more calming and balancing effect. Obviously, if there's a lack of fire or if Mars is weak then we *would* use red and other bright, warm colours to stimulate energy and enthusiasm.

The same goes for the aromatherapy oils. We wouldn't give a stimulating oil such as rosemary to someone whose mind can't stop racing, but for the person whose mind is sluggish or confused it would be the ideal choice.

Although it may be productive to try the remedies mentioned for your particular conditions, I would also recommend you use your own intuition as to which therapies and remedies will work best for you, because ultimately your higher self knows better than anyone else what you need for your own well-being.

1

Astrology and the Four Levels of Well-being

'All disease originates in the mind. Nothing appears in the body unless there is a mental pattern corresponding to it.'
DR JOSEPH MURPHY, *The Power of the Unconscious Mind*

To many people, health is a physical thing. We think that if we feed our bodies correctly, exercise them occasionally and don't subject them to too much stress, we'll remain hale and hearty. While this certainly helps, it is only a small factor in the creation of health and well-being. We also need to nourish ourselves emotionally, psychologically and spiritually. Unfortunately, this is where conventional medicine falls flat on its face for it has no answer to emotional, psychological or spiritual malaise, and yet the root cause of almost all our physical problems can be found at one of these three levels. Our physical bodies are the final, outer manifestation of what is going on at an inner level.

This being the case, we need to be able to understand this inner level of our being. We have to know ourselves emotionally, mentally and spiritually so that we can prevent the energy imbalances that can cause illness. Think of yourself as a complicated jigsaw puzzle: each of your pieces contains valuable information and reflects part of your whole image, yet it's only when we're expressing each and every one of those pieces that the whole picture becomes visible. Your natal chart depicts each one of your pieces. Your Sun in Pisces shows that you function best as a caring compassionate being, but your Moon in Aries shows that you also need to be operating in a courageous, dynamic, original way. Another piece of the puzzle may be Mars in Cancer revealing a need for domestic security, but which is actually masking a deep emotional insecurity. If Mars is squaring Neptune, we have another piece of the puzzle but it's only when these individual pieces of information are slotted together that we see the total unique image that is you.

An understanding of your natal chart can give you an understanding of who you are, and once you know who you are you can live more harmoniously with yourself.

When used from this holistic perspective, astrology can help us to identify and transform the following factors that can create disease:

O imbalances of energy

O suppressed or denied emotions

O denied or frustrated needs

O areas of low self-worth

O blockages and negative patterns

O lack of purpose

O negative or self-limiting attitudes or beliefs

Before we move on to look at how the chart can reveal predisposition towards illness, let's take a deeper look at how an energy imbalance at the spiritual, mental and emotional levels of our being can filter down to cause physical problems, and which planets relate to which level.

Spiritual well-being

Perhaps the most important of the three levels is the spiritual level, because this is where it all starts. If we are fulfilled and at peace at the very centre of our being, it radiates outwards, having an equally positive and peaceful effect on our minds and ultimately our bodies. Unfortunately, though, the spiritual aspect of life is the one that most of western society respects least. We have to make a conscious effort to attend our yoga classes or devote 20 minutes a day to silence or meditation, while in the East the spiritual aspect of life is as normal and vital as eating. The trouble is, we're simply too busy, which tells much about how far down the list our spiritual well-being comes.

When we experience negative mental or emotional states we can often see the effect upon our health – sometimes immediately, as in the case of the 'angry migraine', the 'nervous tummy' or the 'stressed-out skin condition'. However, we don't seem to make the same connection on a spiritual level when experiencing a lack of meaning or purpose and the accompanying sense of frustration, unhappiness or depression. These states of being, if experienced for long enough, may well eventually damage our health.

When we neglect ourselves spiritually we are usually disconnected from who we really are, the results of which can be lack of purpose and meaninglessness, an overly busy lifestyle that keeps us from slowing down enough to look within, or an overly material approach to life where the hole within needs constant feeding with material goods or exciting experiences. To reconnect with our spiritual centre we could take a walk in nature, meditate, or spend some time alone with ourselves to determine what we really want and need. To nourish the spiritual self we need to be living out who we came here to be, and to acknowledge that there is a higher power to which we are all connected.

We all have a unique path in life, a destiny to fulfil, and yet so many of us wander from this path and become lost and confused. What did we come here to do? What is our purpose? What really fulfils us? Does our life have meaning? Asking these vitally important questions can lead us towards spiritual fulfilment and give us a real zest for life. Dr Robert Leichtman sums it up nicely when he says that 'the purpose of the body is to express the light of the soul'.

The planets governing our spiritual nature are the Sun, Jupiter and Neptune.

All in the mind

How we are at the spiritual level filters down to our mind. If we are out of touch with who we are spiritually our mind won't be at peace. It is in the mind that our beliefs and attitudes are formed, which in turn govern how we feel about ourselves and how we act emotionally. If we hold negative beliefs about ourselves in some way, we will hold ourselves back and this can then lead to frustration and resentment as we see others having or being what we secretly long to have or be.

Problems at the mental level can range from simple anxiety and a worrisome mind (usually depicted in the chart via difficult aspects to Mercury), to serious fears and complexes (usually shown by Saturn and sometimes by Pluto). What has become apparent to me while studying the planets in relation to health is the frequency with which Mercury and especially Saturn appear in a negative context. Saturn reveals where we are most insecure and fearful, while Mercury shows how we think. Difficult aspects to Mercury can create anxiety, worry and a restless mind, and a troublesome Saturn can leave us overly fearful. Hardly surprising, then, that during my research of the Bach flower remedies in conjunction with planetary aspects, the one scoring the biggest 'hit' was Mercury aspecting Saturn.

The planets governing our mental state are Mercury, Saturn, Uranus and Pluto.

Identifying emotional needs

The natal chart can show the physical weak spots in the body, but more importantly it can reveal our potential for the toxic emotions that lead to the weak spots. Emotional well-being is essential if we are to be healthy. Most of us have noticed that when emotionally upset, whether because of anger, hurt, despondency, fear or shock, we are much more likely to go down with a cold or flu or, if already unwell, we may notice that our symptoms worsen. By being aware of our emotional tendencies and working on them, we can understand why we react in ways that are ultimately damaging.

The biggest astrological clue to our emotional responses can be found by studying the position of our Moon. A strongly placed Moon will reveal a person who can express feelings easily and feel good about taking care of his or her own needs as well as the needs of others. Likewise, if we want to see how someone expresses anger, we would look to his or her Mars. If Mars is placed in an outgoing sign and has no difficult aspects, anger will be expressed much more healthily than someone who has Mars in a sign that leans towards suppression. If this person's Mars also suffers from inhibiting aspects, we would perhaps expect his or her anger to be channelled inwards, with damaging results. If our Mars isn't particularly well placed, we will need to find an alternative way of channelling our energy – martial arts or meditation for example.

The planets governing our emotional states are the Moon, Venus and Mars.

2

Astrological Signposts

*'By analysing the natal horoscope, we can determine
how to harmonise our physical vehicles so that we
may walk in balance on the Earth Mother.'*
MARCIA STARCK, *Healing with Astrology*

The important question to ask when studying a chart from a health perspective is, where are the imbalances of energy? Since good health results from a state of balance and harmony we can use the chart to assess how balanced a person is likely to be and where his or her greatest areas of tension lie. It is also important to remember that a 'difficult' chart does not necessarily predispose one towards ill health and unhappiness, it merely offers potentials and reveals challenges. Whether or not we rise to meet these challenges depends on how self-aware we are and how vigilant we are with our own weaknesses.

So where do we begin to look for these energy imbalances?

Signs and elements

If we want to gain an overall view of a person's health, we would start by assessing the balance of elements. Imbalances within the four elements – air, fire, earth and water – can reveal our tendencies towards ailments and their likely causes. Someone with little or no fire in his or her chart may have poor digestion and feel the cold more than others. Such a person would benefit from eating spices and warming herbs, and taking more exercise. Someone with excess air would need to take care of his or her system and may benefit from eating calming foods such as oats, and taking up a relaxing pastime such as meditation or yoga. Someone who was low in earth signs or planets would need grounding, and so spending time in nature and doing physical things such as gardening and cooking would restore the balance.

THE ELEMENTS
The air signs: Gemini, Libra, Aquarius
The earth signs: Taurus, Virgo, Capricorn
The fire signs: Aries, Leo, Sagittarius
The water signs: Cancer, Scorpio, Pisces

Cardinal, fixed and mutable signs

Just as we can divide the 12 signs into the four elements, we can also divide them again into three main groups – cardinal, fixed and mutable, otherwise known as the quadruplicities. These three groups have different ways of expressing energy and, since illness occurs due to an imbalance of energy, we can determine why we become ill by understanding how we express our energy. While your Sun sign is relevant, it is also important to assess the overall balance of quadruplicities. For example, you may be a mutable Pisces, but if you have your Moon and Ascendant in Taurus, you may be more fixed than mutable.

The cardinal signs: Aries, Cancer, Libra, Capricorn

If you are a cardinal sign you have a strong energy that you need to learn to use constructively, or it may turn to bossiness, aggression or frustration. These in turn can lead to infections, contagious illnesses, ME and accidents as you fail to recognise your limits. With these signs, you may need to learn to let go of the need to be someone and recognise that you already are someone, regardless of achievements, family, relationships or career. Meditation will help you to reflect, and martial arts or a sport will help channel your forceful energy in a constructive manner.

The fixed signs: Taurus, Leo, Scorpio, Aquarius

If you are a fixed sign you have a stable kind of energy, but often have difficulty in adapting to change and letting go – not just physically, but also of old emotions, thoughts, beliefs and habits. If you hold on too much, you may suffer from congestion, growths, cysts, tumours and blockages. You would ideally be suited to physical therapies such as deep body massage and rolfing, both of which help the body expel accumulated toxins. Dance, singing and tai-chi will free your fixed energy and help you to be more flowing and adaptable.

The mutable signs: Gemini, Virgo, Sagittarius, Pisces

The mutable signs have a very fluid energy and so you can easily adapt to change. You do, however, need grounding and relaxing as your energy tends to be scattered and easily distracted, so walking, gardening, yoga, deep breathing and meditation would be ideal. Since you have a delicate mental state and are easily worried, the gentle therapies such as Bach flower remedies, aromatherapy and homoeopathy would be particularly suitable for you. You may also find that having a bottle of rescue remedy on hand is particularly useful to calm your delicate nerves.

Planets and health

Before embarking upon further chart analysis, it is useful to have an understanding of the function of the ten planets. Each of these planets represents a particular type of energy and governs the anatomical or physiological function shown.

Planet	Represents	Anatomy and physiology
The Sun	Our vital energy and consciousness	Heart and spine
The Moon	Our emotions and unconscious	Breasts, stomach, bodily fluids, mucus, fertility
Mercury	Our intellect and communication	Breathing, the mental system, speech, hearing
Venus	Our creativity, relating and balance	Hormone function, kidneys, homeostasis, ovaries
Mars	Our drive and assertiveness	Muscles, inflammation, sex drive, immune system
Jupiter	Our self-belief and ability to grow	Liver, fat metabolism, blood, growth hormones

Planet	Represents	Anatomy and physiology
Saturn	Our fears, insecurities and structure	Bones, teeth, hair, skin, joints, the structure of our body
Uranus	Our individuality and intuition	Nervous system, rhythmic pulsation, co-ordination
Neptune	Our spirituality and imagination	Pineal gland, right-brain function, appendix, osmosis
Pluto	Our dark side and transformation	Elimination, reproductive organs, regenerative ability

When working harmoniously, we have good health, but if for any reason one or more planets are struggling to let their energy flow as it should, our health may be compromised. The reasons why a planetary energy may be blocked are varied, but the following might be seen as the biggest stumbling blocks.

Homesick planets

Just as people, animals and plants function better in some environments than in others, so too do planets flourish in some signs but struggle in others. The two technical terms for a planet in a sign alien to its basic nature are 'fall' and 'detriment'. When a planet thrives in a sign it is known to be 'exalted'. It is also very happy in the sign that it rules (rulership). Mars, for example, rules Aries and so, while it is happy here in its own sign, it is also comfortable in the other fire signs since it is able to express its energy in a similar way. However, if we put the outgoing feisty Mars in a gentle introverted water sign such as Cancer (its fall), we have problems. Mars doesn't have a clue how to express itself here for its masculine, driving personality is dampened by the sensitive, nurturing, watery nature of Cancer. Similarly, Mars in its detriment sign of Libra struggles to express its aggressive energy in such a peace-loving sign. In Capricorn, though, Mars is exalted because the steady ambition and persistence of this sign is able to make the most of the powerful Mars energy.

When several planets are 'homesick', it can put a strain on the health, as much of the person's energy is fighting against itself. It is particularly important in these cases that the individual finds constructive ways of expressing the energy of the weakened planet, perhaps by using remedies that strengthen that planet. A weakened Mars, for example, would benefit from iron supplements, the colour red, exercise, and the Mars aromatherapy oils such as basil and black pepper.

Check the table on the next page to see how many of your planets are exalted or in fall or detriment.

Planet		Rules	Exalted	Detriment	Fall
☉	Sun	Leo	Aries	Aquarius	Libra
☽	Moon	Cancer	Taurus	Capricorn	Scorpio
☿	Mercury	Gemini/Virgo	Virgo	Sagittarius	Pisces
♀	Venus	Libra/Taurus	Pisces	Aries	Virgo
♂	Mars	Aries	Capricorn	Libra	Cancer
♃	Jupiter	Sagittarius	Cancer	Gemini	Capricorn
♄	Saturn	Capricorn	Libra	Cancer	Aries
♅	Uranus	Aquarius	Scorpio	Leo	Taurus
♆	Neptune	Pisces	Leo	Virgo	Aquarius
♇	Pluto	Scorpio	Virgo	Taurus	Pisces

Difficult aspects

The second and perhaps most intense weakening factor upon a planet is when it receives stressful aspects from other planets. An aspect occurs when two planets form an angle to each other such as a 90° angle (square) or a 120° angle (trine). It is generally regarded that the tense or hard aspects are the squares, oppositions and quincunx. The conjunction can also be classed as a hard aspect when the planets involved have little in common, such as Mars conjunct Saturn or Saturn conjunct Neptune. The easy or soft aspects are the trines and sextiles. These easy aspects don't normally cause health problems because the energy is flowing rather than blocked. However, the passive nature of such aspects can sometimes create problems, especially if the two planets in question lean towards laziness or excess, as in the case of Jupiter aspects to the Sun, the Moon, Venus or Neptune.

Just as with humans, the planets have other planets that they favour or get on with, and others that they can't get on with at all. When two planets clash and the aspect formed between them is a hard one, the result can be tremendous internal stress and, as we know, prolonged stress is a major cause of illness. When looking to create well-being, we would take note of the hard aspects and try to balance the stressful energies. When a planet receives more than one hard aspect – especially if the other planets involved 'don't get on with it' – this planet's energy is usually weakened and needs strengthening.

Because the planets are constantly moving it is also possible to see when the periods of greatest stress will be, how long they will last, and the best way of responding to the stress. These planetary movements, otherwise known as transits, can be instrumental in triggering the onset of a disease or symptom, so it's as well to know when the stressful transits will strike. (For more on this subject see Chapter 13 on transits.)

The houses

Astrologers divide the chart into 12 segments, otherwise known as houses. Each house relates to a specific area of life, and planets within such a house are able to shed much light on how we operate within this area. A house containing several planets will have particular interest to the individual, who may focus a great deal of his or her energies in that area. As with signs and aspects, each planet is more comfortable in some houses and less so in others.

Houses are important because they reveal in which areas of life we will be most likely to face difficulties. The houses and their areas of life are as follows:

THE 1ST HOUSE   – The self, appearance, outer personality, new beginnings

THE 2ND HOUSE   – Money, possessions, values, self-worth

THE 3RD HOUSE   – Short travel, communication, education, siblings, intellect

THE 4TH HOUSE   – The home and family, our childhood and roots, parents (usually the mother), the unconscious and the past

THE 5TH HOUSE   – Fun, creativity, romance, love affairs, animals, children, gambling and risk-taking, sport, being ourselves

THE 6TH HOUSE   – Health, work, service, duty, small pets

THE 7TH HOUSE   – Relationships, marriage, legal matters

THE 8TH HOUSE   – Sex, death, loss, transformation, intimacy, birth, wealth, inheritance

THE 9TH HOUSE   – Foreign travel, higher education, philosophy, religion, beliefs

THE 10TH HOUSE   – Career, vocation, success, public acclaim, parents (usually the father)

THE 11TH HOUSE   – Friends, groups, social life, society, charity, vision and dreams

THE 12TH HOUSE   – Secrets, karma, spirituality, endings, seclusion, institutions, inner journeys

From a health point of view, we look to the 6th and 12th houses when looking for problems and indicators. While it may seem obvious to look to the 6th house, this being the house of health, the 12th may not seem quite so apparent. In my work with clients I have noticed time and time again that people with planets in the 12th house who aren't focusing on their inner selves and taking note of their spiritual side become ill. In these cases, the requirements of the planet – which are largely spiritual and inwardly focused – aren't being met. This is also where we reap what we've sown, and if we've led a largely hedonistic or selfish life this can return to us in the form of illness as a stark reminder that the soul needs some nourishment too.

Although houses are important in health analysis they don't have the same bearing upon our well-being as the aspects do and for that reason we will only make occasional reference to them. It is still advisable though to have an understanding of your planets in their houses so that you can know where your energies should be directed for maximum happiness and fulfilment.

Now that we have seen how the planets and signs can help or hinder us in creating health and well-being, let's take a more detailed look at each one of the planets to understand what they are asking of us.

3

The Sun – Your Vital Force

*'There is a vitality, a life force, an energy, a
quickening, that is translated through you into
action, and because there is only one of you in all
time, this expression is unique.'*
MARTHA GRAHAM

How do you feel when the Sun shines? If you're like most people, your mood will be brighter than it is on a dull day. Perhaps you feel more optimistic, more energetic, more keen to get on and do things. And yet, when the Sun is intense, it can make us feel lazy. We want to bask in its rays, soak up its energy and just relax.

Because the Sun can have such a dramatic effect on our moods, it may come as no surprise to learn that the Sun in our astrological charts is granted huge importance – especially the role it plays in our physical health. The Sun is fundamental to our health and well-being, for it represents the real us – the centre of our being. From the Sun all life springs and it is the same within our birth charts. It represents our drive, our creativity and our enthusiasm for life itself.

The Sun and your unique expression

In order to remain healthy and happy, we must express our Sun, for to do so means we are expressing our inner light or radiance. If your Sun is in Aries then, you must be able to make your mark in some way and do it with enthusiasm, courage and originality. With the Sun in Taurus you are here to develop security and build steadily and methodically upon what you have. Of course, you're far more than just a Sun sign, so you will also need to express the house position of your Sun and its aspects. If, for example, you have Neptune conjunct your Sun, you have a strongly Pisces element to your nature – soft, caring, compassionate – and would ideally express this through your work or hobbies.

The sign, house position and aspects to your Sun reflect your unique qualities that are burning to be expressed. To not be aware of, or to repress, who we really are is akin to a powerful light bulb never being switched on.

A strongly placed Sun will usually indicate good health and a strong constitution (all other chart factors being equal) because its energy is able to be easily expressed. Conversely, the Sun in a weak part of the chart can result in low energy and a greater susceptibility to illness.

Physiological correspondences

The areas of the body that correspond to the Sun are primarily the heart and back. It also has links with our immunity and governs consciousness, vitality and the eyes.

The heart

The Sun rules the heart – the centre of our being and the life-giving organ. The heart works tirelessly 24 hours a day to supply our bodies with the essential nutrients carried in our blood. Symbolically our heart represents joy and love – our capacity to feel it and to give it. The Sun and its counterparts – Leo and the 5th house – are all about radiating and shining. Here we don't try to do or be anything, we just are, with childlike simplicity, and maybe this is partly why heart disease is now the number one killer in western society. We are so busy doing, striving, achieving and overcomplicating our lives that we have forgotten how to 'be'. This capacity to just be is a very spiritual orientation, which is why the position of the Sun in our charts can have such a strong effect on our happiness. If we are not happy at our core centre, at the deepest, most spiritual level of our being, this will radiate out through the other three layers – the psychological, the emotional and the physical, just as the blood from our heart radiates out to every last millimetre of our body.

Heart problems then can be viewed as a deep inner discontent. We are being blocked in some way from shining our true light and we are disconnected from our intuitive, feeling side. This blockage can be a suppression of emotions, but more commonly it is caused by anger, which is the biggest block to peace and happiness. This is why type A personalities – the aggressive, competitive go-getters with short fuses – are far more prone to heart attacks than their peaceful, passive type B counterparts. The heart simply cannot process anger on a continual basis, nor can it cope with the coldness, colourlessness and lack of empathy that is so marked in the competitive, striving elements of our society today. The heart is intuitive – 'listen to your heart' and ' go with your heart' are common phrases, yet how often do we follow such advice? The heart knows, and every time we override it with logic and rationality, we make it shrink a little more. It is often people who have lost this connection to their intuition, to their feelings and compassion that will have heart difficulties.

What we need to do, then, is create more of a balance between our heads and our hearts; then we might find our heart won't have to shout so much to let itself be heard.

Living in harmony with the Sun – intuition, creativity and simplicity

To live in harmony with the Sun in our chart, we first need to understand what it is asking of us. For example, someone with the Sun in his or her 5th house needs to be creative, artistic or sporty, or find other ways to have fun, whereas someone with the Sun in the 11th house needs to have an active and varied social life. The sign and aspects to our Sun will add further information, all combining to create a detailed and unique portrait of how we should be manifesting our solar energy.

Intuition

We need to honour our Sun by getting in touch with our hearts and finding out who we really are. We need to pay attention to our inner promptings and listen to our intuition. The more attention we pay to our intuition, the easier it will be to understand it. Men in particular need to develop this aspect of themselves because, in spite of their efforts to integrate their feminine side with their masculinity, there is still immense pressure on them to achieve, which can drown out their inner promptings of what they really want. This isn't to say that women aren't susceptible to heart problems too. Indeed it is something they need to be vigilant for in our increasingly competitive society. But because they are naturally more in tune with their feelings and intuition, heart problems are less frequent in women.

Creativity and play

The Sun is a creative life force. We each have the Sun somewhere in our charts, therefore we have each been blessed with an element of this creativity and we should use it. When we are being creative, we are once again like children – playful and in the moment. The more creativity we can bring into our lives, the healthier we will be.

Simplicity

The Sun is simple in its behaviour. It shines. End of story. Children too just shine. Unfortunately, as adults we lose this ability to just enjoy the moment of whatever we're doing. We are always thinking of the next thing to do and consequently, what could be a joyous hour or moment becomes tainted by the clutter in our mind. Meditation, yoga and tai-chi can help us clear some space in our minds so that we are more able to be in the moment. We are then more able to get pleasure from the most simple of tasks. We also need to guard against cluttering our lives, as this will be symbolic of the complications in our mental and emotional states. Think of ways in which you can pare down your life: do we really need 24 television channels, two cars, three different loans to pay off, designer clothes and all the latest gadgets to make us feel we're achieving something? Keep your life simple and you will be happier for it.

Your Sun is out of balance when:

○ You think the world revolves around you

○ You expect special treatment

○ You take people for granted and don't notice what they do for you

○ You neglect the people closest to you

○ You expect applause for your efforts rather than doing something for the love of it

○ You feel that achievement equates with success

○ You become unhappy or frustrated if someone else is getting more attention than you

To increase the strength of your Sun and health of your heart:

- ○ Practise peaceful meditation
- ○ Do something creative or fun at least once a week
- ○ Become aware of any anger and resolve to let it go
- ○ Find a hobby or interest that centres you
- ○ Incorporate the colour orange into your life, through your clothes, food or décor
- ○ Discover and live out your unique purpose: everyone has a reason for being – what's yours?
- ○ Let go of the need to strive, achieve and compete; there is nothing wrong with achieving things, but if it becomes a need rather than a by-product of love for what you're doing, it is unhealthy
- ○ Create as much simplicity as you can; let go of clutter – mentally, emotionally and physically
- ○ Recover your childlike spirit, play a game, paint a picture, see the beauty in as many things as you can
- ○ Develop your compassion for all living things – the heart wants to give not take

Aspects to the Sun (including transits)

Sun–Moon

KEYWORDS: Inner conflict

Since these two planets are essentially opposites, we might expect that difficult aspects between them would have a corresponding effect on the health. In actual fact, the energies of these two planets combined are quite mild, but the hard aspects can lead a person to feel very uncomfortable within themselves which, if emotionally painful enough, could lead to physical problems. Having said that, the worst of this aspect usually relates to eye or fluid problems.

HERBS AND SPICES: eyebright, juniper

BACH FLOWERS: agrimony, cerato

COLOUR: green

AROMATHERAPY OILS: chamomile, geranium, jasmine, melissa, ylang ylang

Sun–Mercury

KEYWORDS: The bright spark

When Mercury aspects the Sun, everything is speeded up – metabolism, thoughts, reactions and speech. Mercury can either stimulate the Sun or it can bring nervousness and an inability to switch off and relax. People with this combination may live in their head and so need to find ways to ground themselves. Earthy physical pursuits are best such as walking, gardening, cooking, woodwork, needlework and pottery.

HERBS AND SPICES: valerian, vervain

BACH FLOWERS: cerato, heather, impatiens

COLOURS: green, pink, turquoise

AROMATHERAPY OILS: chamomile, lavender, neroli, vetivert

Sun–Venus

KEYWORD: Indulgence

Venus aspects to the Sun have very little detrimental effect on the health, other than a love of sweet foods that can lead to weight gain and dental problems. There can be a passive element to the personality, and if this isn't balanced by more invigorating chart factors it could lead to apathy and laziness.

HERBS AND SPICES: ginger, ginseng

BACH FLOWERS: chicory, clematis

COLOURS: orange, red, yellow

AROMATHERAPY OILS: basil, benzoin, rosemary

Sun–Mars

KEYWORD: Competitive

Physically speaking, even the stressful aspects between the Sun and Mars have a protective effect on health, because Mars is the ruler of the immune system. Therefore, any aspect governing immunity (Mars) and our overall physical function (the Sun) will be positive. The benefits of this aspect kick in when the health is under attack as the body's defences will be very quick to react. This means that minor conditions – especially infections – can be overcome quickly. However, on a psychological level, the hard aspects can indicate an over-competitive nature and a propensity towards anger, irritation and impatience, which can have a stressful effect on physical well-being, particularly on the heart. Therefore, Sun–Mars people need to practise patience, tolerance and tranquillity. All relaxing disciplines such as yoga, tai-chi and meditation would have a positive effect. However, these practises on their own would probably not be enough for the energy and competitive drive of these people, so a combination of one of these spiritual practices and a sport such as football or tennis would be ideal.

Because there is a strong competitive element to this aspect, the need to strive and achieve at all costs should be guarded against. It is important for these people to have a challenge, but if their self-esteem is built upon the need to be successful, they will forever be chasing their tails.

HERBS AND SPICES: chamomile, garlic, valerian, yarrow

BACH FLOWERS: heather, impatiens, vine

COLOURS: pale green, pastels, pink, turquoise

AROMATHERAPY OILS: chamomile, geranium, jasmine, marjoram, rose

VITAMINS AND MINERALS: copper, vitamin E

Sun–Jupiter

KEYWORDS: Big is beautiful

Aspects between the Sun and Jupiter – even the hard aspects – have a relatively mild effect upon health, the main problem being over-indulgence. When Jupiter contacts the Sun, everything is big, fun, optimistic and a little on the arrogant side. These are the aspects, then, of those who eat, drink or smoke too much, but who refuse to listen to well-meaning advice, believing that they'll be okay, because Sun–Jupiter people never believe that anything bad will happen to them. Of course it can, though such optimism often has a protective effect. However, it would be prudent (not an approach easily adhered to by Sun–Jupiter types) to guard against physical excess and over-indulgence, otherwise liver problems may well arise.

HERBS AND SPICES: dandelion root, fennel, milkthistle

BACH FLOWERS: heather, water violet

COLOURS: cream, pale blue, white, yellow

AROMATHERAPY OILS: fennel, geranium

PHILOSOPHY: less is more

Sun–Saturn

KEYWORD: Melancholy

To have Saturn aspecting the Sun poses something of a challenge. These planets do not make easy companions: Saturn is cold, restrictive, fearful, cautious, insecure and regimented; the Sun is the opposite of these things. If Saturn forms a hard aspect to your Sun you may find that have to take steps to increase your energy and protect your health. Saturn can be very draining on the Sun's energy, so your first priority is plenty of sleep, followed by a good healthy diet with plenty of protein and calcium. Exercise is essential to maintain energy levels and create a positive state of mind, since Saturn will also have a negative effect on the levels of optimism.

Traditionally, this aspect is associated with back, hair, skin and teeth problems and bone weakness. Psychologically, this aspect can induce melancholy, with a belief or feeling that life is hard. Effort needs to be made to focus on the good things, and to see life's trials as growth-inducing opportunities for the soul.

Learning to focus on the beauty of the world will be of tremendous benefit, so keeping a daily gratitude journal is ideal for Sun–Saturn people.

With this aspect, the Sun is weak, so pay particular attention to the pointers below to increase its strength.

HERBS AND SPICES: garlic, ginger, nettle, pepper, prickly ash

BACH FLOWERS: elm, larch, mimulus, mustard, oak, olive, pine, rock water, vine, water violet, wild rose, willow

COLOURS: gold, orange, red, yellow

AROMATHERAPY OILS: bergamot, benzoin, clary sage, melissa, neroli, orange, rose, ylang ylang

VITAMINS AND MINERALS: calcium, chondroitin, glucosamine, iron, phosphorus, sulphur, vitamin C, zinc

Sun–Uranus

KEYWORDS: The unique soul

The positive side of a Sun–Uranus aspect is one of lively stimulation. The downside, however, is hyperactivity, nervousness and an inability to relax. Uranus will increase the tempo of the Sun, but its energy is likely to be sporadic, therefore situations that require endurance and patience are likely to be met with disdain. Uranus governs the rhythms of the body and electrical impulses. When aspected to the Sun, there can be heart defects such as irregularities and murmurs. Spasms, cramps, tremors and tics are also possible side-effects of a Sun–Uranus aspect.

Psychologically, an inability to relax may need to be dealt with.

The watchword with this aspect is 'grounding'. If you have a tense aspect between these two planets you will need to find ways to ground yourself as Uranus will incline you to being spaced out or hyperactive. Walking is ideal, as are gardening and cooking. A massage will bring you back into your body and help you focus on your physical senses. Any practical or physical task that brings you back down to earth will alleviate the worst of this aspect.

HERBS AND SPICES: chamomile, motherwort, valerian

BACH FLOWERS: impatiens, star of Bethlehem, vervain, walnut, water violet

COLOURS: blue, green, turquoise

AROMATHERAPY OILS: chamomile, lavender, marjoram, neroli, patchouli, sage

VITAMINS AND MINERALS: copper, magnesium, manganese, vitamin E

IDEAL THERAPIES: aromatherapy massage, meditation

Sun–Neptune

KEYWORDS: Identity crisis

When Neptune aspects the Sun we can either be full of inspiration, creativity and idealism, or we can suffer from escapism, confusion and deception (our own or at the hands of others). Neptune aspects to the Sun, either natally or via a transit, seek to dissolve our barriers between ourselves and the rest of the world. If we consider ourselves to be very rational and like everything black or white and clear cut, such an ambiguous aspect can prove to be very troubling as our tight grip on reality begins to corrode under Neptune's dissolving waters. We may be unsure of our purpose in life – we may even be unsure of who we really are, as Neptune blurs the distinctions and makes it difficult to identify where one thing ends and another begins. In Neptune's world, all is one.

On a physical level then, Sun–Neptune aspects can manifest as lowered immunity, revealing at a psychological level an inability to differentiate between 'me' and 'the other'. This can result in allergies and repeated infections. Creating a stronger identity can help create a stronger immune system. A need to escape from harsh reality can result in alcohol or drug abuse, but any habit that creates apathy or reduces the focus of oneself or one's life needs to be avoided. Television – especially soaps – can be a socially acceptable drug that encourages us to focus on other people's lives instead of constructively dealing with our own.

Eye problems, especially poor vision, can mirror a reluctance to face reality and look to the future, or may reveal our lack of clarity about where we're going.

HERBS AND SPICES: echinacea, garlic, goldenseal, nettle

BACH FLOWERS: clematis, olive, pine, rock rose, scleranthus, wild oat, wild rose

COLOURS: brown, green, indigo, orange

AROMATHERAPY OILS: frankincense, myrrh, rosemary, tea tree, vetivert

VITAMINS AND MINERALS: co-enzyme Q10, iron, selenium, vitamins A, C, E, zinc

Sun–Pluto

KEYWORD: INTENSITY

When Pluto joins forces with the Sun, a powerful reaction is formed. In the natal chart, such an aspect gives a certain intensity to the character that needs to find some kind of an outlet – particularly if the aspect is a hard one. Without a suitable outlet for this powerful energy and without awareness, this aspect can create problems, largely because the energy will be turned in on itself. Physically, Sun–Pluto aspects are associated with growths, swellings, cysts, lumps, blockages and tumours, which on a psychological level reflect a holding on and an inability to let go. On the positive side, all Sun–Pluto aspects, but especially the soft aspects, indicate great regenerative healing powers.

To ensure good health with this aspect, we need to be able to let go and practise forgiveness.

HERBS AND SPICES: burdock, dandelion root, vervain, yellow dock root

BACH FLOWERS: heather, holly, sweet chestnut, willow

COLOURS: magenta, pink, turquoise, white

AROMATHERAPY OILS: fennel, geranium, juniper, lavender, rose

VITAMINS AND MINERALS: selenium, vitamin E

4

The Moon –
Your Inner Self

'When we truly care for ourselves, it becomes
possible to care more profoundly about other people.
The more alert we are to our own needs, the more
loving and generous we can be toward others.'
EDA LESHAN

Perhaps the most noticeable thing about the Moon, apart from its luminous beauty, is that it is forever changing. The Moon is in a constant state of flux, ebbing and flowing, and perhaps this is why it is connected with our feelings and emotional natures, which can change from one day or even hour to the next and which we feel we are powerless to control. We may wake up grumpy one day and perky the next; or may feel a surge of jealousy or anger at one time but deal with the same situation in a calm manner another time.

The Moon governs our unconscious, our hidden motivations, our needs and desires. The Moon in our charts is therefore important because it can show us what we are unconsciously suppressing. Indeed, some medical astrologers believe that, of all the planets, the Moon has the strongest impact on our health. This makes sense because a weak or difficult Moon may reveal trouble in expressing feelings, and suppressing our emotions is often the quickest way to become ill.

The Moon and our inner child

The Moon in our charts can offer insights into our emotional states and where things might have gone wrong during childhood. Because the Moon is instinctive and has no rational powers, what we experienced as children becomes ingrained by the time we're teenagers, so we will tend to react automatically to a situation that triggers an old memory. This subjective response means we are unable to see the situation as it really is: it may not be appropriate as an adult to behave in a clingy manner when our partner wants to go away for a weekend on his or her own, but if we suffered any kind of loss or abandonment as a child, then this may well be our response. This is why difficulties with the Moon in our charts are the hardest to deal with, because we cannot apply rational thought to them. We cannot reason with our Moon when it's feeling hurt or threatened, just as we cannot comfort a distraught child with reasoning – only a hug will do. Likewise, the only way we can overcome a painful emotional issue is to heal the original wound and nurture our inner child.

In order to see where your inner child is hurting, check out the stressful aspects of your Moon – for example, the Moon tensely aspecting Saturn may reveal a lack of early love and nurturing. The Moon aspecting Pluto might well indicate a painful trauma such as a loss, whilst a hard lunar aspect to Neptune may point to confusion and a lack of identity.

Physiological correspondences

The Moon rules our fluids, secretions, mucous membranes and tears, the menstrual cycle, breasts and stomach. The fluids are representative of emotions, the breasts reflect our capacity to nurture and our stomach is where we take in nourishment.

Fluids and emotions

Let's look at the fluids in the body first. Problems with fluids such as water retention show us that we are not going with the flow, or that we are blocking or holding on to certain feelings. As children, we are able to let go of past pain and don't dwell too much on what happened yesterday, never mind last week or last month. But as adults, we can live in the past if we are prone to guilt or if we feel that the present or the future doesn't have much to offer. We are also good at nursing old hurts and apportioning blame and feeling resentful of the mistakes that we made and the hurt that others have caused. By hanging on to these negative feelings we are sowing the seeds for future physical problems, and so learning to let go and forgive is very important. One sign that we're not doing this is if we manifest blockages or swellings containing fluid, such as water on the knee and cysts. These are sure signs that we're holding on to some kind of negative emotion and need to let it go.

The breasts and nurturing

The breasts or chest reflect the area where we give love and nurturing. Problems here usually reflect too much nurturing of others combined with a lack of self-nurturing. Are you too concerned with the needs of others at the expense of your own? Strong lunar types (Cancer Sun, Moon or Ascendant, Moon in the 7th or 10th houses) can find themselves so attentive to the needs of other people that they become resentful at not having their own needs met. Likewise, reflecting other people's brilliance is not really the answer to a fulfilling life. We need to support others while acknowledging that we have a life to live too. By finding a balance between nurturing both ourselves and others, difficulties in the breast area can be alleviated.

The stomach and nourishment

The stomach is governed by the Moon (and the sign of Cancer) because this is where we receive our nourishment, and food has a very strong relationship with our emotions. We all know people who binge on chocolates and cakes when feeling down, and diseases such as anorexia are born from an intense dislike of the self. If we're not good enough then we won't feed ourselves properly – we won't show ourselves the love and nurturing that, hopefully, our mothers gave us when we were babies. Many children, though, are punished by the withholding of food – 'you'll go to bed without your supper' being a classic – or, at the other extreme, are pacified or 'bought' with sweets and goodies. In this case the sweets are acting as a replacement for love and affection. Likewise, dairy products represent nurturing, and many of us find milky products quite soothing and reassuring – a bowl of rice pudding takes us straight back to childhood.

Understanding our relationship with food creates awareness of how we relate to ourselves. Do you feel guilty when reaching for the chocolate cake? Do you stop eating when depressed, or do you binge on all the things you know are bad for you? What are your favourite groups of food – sweet, dairy, spicy? To which food groups do you have intolerances? An intolerance to dairy produce such as milk may indicate that you need to seek nurturing from yourself, as opposed to looking for it from outside.

The Moon and the female cycle

The Moon is distinctly feminine in its nature, and so governs the menstrual cycle. The Moon takes 28 days to go full cycle through the 12 signs, which is of course the normal length of time for a woman's monthly cycle. It stands to reason, then, that any problems with the menstrual cycle and producing children have their roots in issues around being female. There may be a sense of feeling uncomfortable with being a woman or a mother, usually stemming from an event in childhood. Or there may be unresolved issues with the mother herself. Infertility or a reluctance or fear of having children can usually be found in the charts of people with Moon–Saturn or Moon–Pluto aspects. For these women, learning to value their femininity and letting go of fear can be a big step.

Living in harmony with the Moon – acknowledging your inner child

In order to keep the childlike Moon part of ourselves happy, we have to respond to the needs of the child within. We can do this in two ways. Firstly, we need to understand what our inner child needs to feel content and we can identify these needs by recalling what we loved doing as youngsters. Secondly, we need to reassure and comfort our child whenever we're faced with a situation that triggers a negative childhood situation. In other words, we become a parent to ourselves.

Identifying your needs

To get in touch with your Moon and what it needs, think back to your childhood and reflect for a moment on what you really enjoyed doing – perhaps you loved horseriding, playing a sport, going on adventures, writing stories, making things or playing music. Whatever it was (you'll probably be able to think of a handful of things) you need to be doing at least one or two of them now. If what you loved doing as a youngster is too childish, think of ways in which you could bring it into your adult world.

The above exercise will help you identify what you need to do to keep yourself happy and healthy. However, it's also important to identify what your deeper emotional and psychological needs are. Take a piece of paper and write down what your top five needs are. For many people being loved is number one; for others it might be freedom. The need to be creative or playful may feature on your list as you remember how much you used to love doing creative things but for some reason have got out of the habit. Some people have a need to achieve, while others need security. Appreciation, affection or romance may be needs. You may have a need for solitude, or to be in nature, or to travel and explore. Again, thinking back to childhood might help you recognise what your priorities are.

Once you've identified your needs, you'll be able to acknowledge whether these needs are being met or being ignored. If the latter, what can you do to make sure these vital parts of yourself find some fulfilment? If your needs are based on insecurity, such as a need to be seen as special, a need to achieve, a need for appreciation or approval etc., then you may want to look at how and why this need was formed and how you can supply it yourself rather than looking for someone else to fulfil it for you.

Healing your inner child

To overcome deeply rooted emotional issues, such as fear of abandonment, lack of self-love, fear of conflict, neglect or needing to be the best, the adult part of you needs to step back and observe the emotional reaction. Understand that this is the frightened child aspect of yourself, reacting as it did when faced with a similar situation during childhood. You can then do a meditation in which you see your inner child (at the age you were when you first recalled a similar event) and ask it what's wrong. Listen to what your inner child has to say – maybe it's afraid of being left or not loved enough – and then you can embrace the child and give it what it needs. This simple little exercise can have powerful effects.

Going with the emotional flow

The Moon shows us that we need to flow, and that if we are feeling happy we should laugh, if we are feeling sad we should cry, and acknowledge all the various shades of grey in between. To fight our feelings is to deny a part of ourselves. I recently came across the following phrase, 'to feel love for someone but not to share it is like buying a present for someone and not giving it'. Likewise, if we feel angry or upset about something, we need to discuss it immediately to prevent a negative build-up of sour feelings that eventually leads to deep resentment. In this respect, we need to become children again, where feelings are spontaneously and healthily expressed.

Your Moon is out of balance when:

○ You find yourself overeating, bingeing, becoming anorexic or subjecting yourself to any harmful substance

○ You repeatedly find yourself in co-dependent or abusive relationships

○ You cling to people and need others to boost your self-esteem

○ You spend your time running around after others but have little or no time for yourself

○ You spend much of your time clinging to the past and to your memories, both good and bad

○ You use tears or other methods of emotional blackmail to get people to do what you want

To increase the strength of your Moon and emotional well-being:

○ Identify your five strongest needs and if they're not currently being fulfilled, start finding ways to do so now

○ Practise listening to and following your intuition

○ Pay attention to your dreams – perhaps keep a dream diary

○ Make regular time for a little self-nurturing, for instance by making yourself nice meals

○ Become aware of whatever negative thoughts, feelings or memories you may be holding on to and let them go

○ Strengthen your emotional connections with people you love – display photographs of them, let them know how much they mean to you

○ Have someone or something to care for; if you have no children or pets, get a couple of plants and nurture them

○ When you feel a particular emotion, don't try to suppress it; instead, allow it to come and then let it go

○ Vow not to waste your life living in the past – the present is a gift and should be treated as such

○ Treasure your memories – but don't let your life revolve around them

Aspects to the Moon (including transits)
Moon–Sun
See page 31.

Moon–Mercury

KEYWORD: Perception

While not a serious threat to health, this little aspect can induce anxiety and a worrisome nature. This is largely as a result of attitudes picked up in childhood, and anyone with this aspect would do well to question the origins of their beliefs and whether they want to keep them or not. The focus is usually on the past or the family and domestic affairs and much mental energy can be wasted on trivia, the past and gossip. When used constructively, the mind can be very perceptive with a strong intuition present. The worst of this aspect relates to respiratory problems (asthma), and digestive and mental disorders (anxiety), which can largely be countered by developing a more positive, relaxed approach to life.

HERBS AND SPICES: peppermint, sage leaves, skullcap, slippery elm, thyme

BACH FLOWERS: agrimony, aspen, honeysuckle, red chestnut, scleranthus

COLOURS: blue, green, orange, turquoise

AROMATHERAPY OILS: chamomile, fennel, frankincense, geranium, juniper, lavender

VITAMINS AND MINERALS: bioflavanoids, vitamin A, vitamin B complex

Moon–Venus

KEYWORD: Gentleness

This is a very minor aspect in terms of health, and is usually apparent only to women as both these planets govern female functions. Should these two planets be at odds with each other, the result can be menstrual difficulties (PMT etc.) and hormonal troubles. These tend to be reflective of buried issues to do with being female or a mother. Any unhappiness or resentment with being female and all the pressures that the modern woman has to face can lead to disorders of a female nature. Therefore, if female, it is worth looking within to assess what negative messages you might be carrying around as a woman. When you are more comfortable being a woman or a mother, any female troubles should reduce.

The only other possible problem with this combination of gentle, pleasant planets is self-indulgence and laziness. Exercise may be looked upon with disdain, in favour of the box of chocolates and bottle of wine. Needless to say, this can lead to weight problems and all the potential difficulties that lie with being out of condition. Moderation is vital with this combination of planets.

HERBS AND SPICES: dong quai root, evening primrose oil, sage leaves, skullcap

BACH FLOWERS: centaury, chicory, clematis

COLOURS: green, purple

AROMATHERAPY OILS: chamomile, cypress, jasmine, melissa, rose

VITAMINS AND MINERALS: folic acid (for conception), vitamin E

Moon–Mars

KEYWORDS: Emotional angst

When Mars bounces on to the lunar scene, the emotional nature is likely to be tempestuous to say the least. The most common emotion associated with this feisty little aspect is anger. No doubt in childhood there was plenty going on to arouse anger and quite often it seems as though the mother is to blame. However, the past is gone and it does nothing for the health of these people to ruminate on the injustices of the past.

Because of the tendency to lose one's temper, some kind of anger management may need to be learned through either a course or a calming activity such as meditation that helps create a new and more peaceful philosophy. Flying off the handle and stamping one's feet may have worked as a child, but for an adult it will only serve to alienate people and wreak havoc on the health.

Physically, all this churning, angry emotion can result in ulcers, stomach problems and nausea, though people who try and sit on all this energy are more at risk than those who throw regular tantrums. Fevers, headaches and migraines, inflammations and skin eruptions are all signs of angry emotions. Acceptance and tolerance are key traits to develop, followed by patience and the ability to count to ten before reacting.

HERBS AND SPICES: chamomile, feverfew, ginger, peppermint

BACH FLOWERS: beech, holly, impatiens

COLOURS: cream, pale green, pastels, turquoise, white

AROMATHERAPY OILS: benzoin, chamomile, frankincense, lavender, melissa, petitgrain

IDEAL THERAPY: anger management

Moon–Jupiter

KEYWORD: Excess

When the Moon is adversely aspected by Jupiter the result is often excess in one form or another. Whether this is food (a sweet tooth, inclining the person towards goodies – and plenty of them), alcohol, drugs, sleep or whatever, is largely irrelevant, for the form of excess is merely mirroring the individual's excessive personality and lack of direction. Moderation needs to be adopted otherwise the liver will struggle to metabolise fats, which can then lead to a whole range of problems including sickness and headaches. Usually with liver problems there is a lack of purpose and the indulgences that the individual loves to partake in fill the inner void that would be automatically filled if he or she could inject more meaning into life – especially the emotional life.

HERBS AND SPICES: burdock, dandelion root, milkthistle

BACH FLOWERS: heather, wild oat

COLOURS: cream, pale green, white, yellow

AROMATHERAPY OILS: eucalyptus, geranium, juniper, pine, rosemary

VITAMINS AND MINERALS: biotin, chromium, potassium

Moon–Saturn

KEYWORD: Insecurity

It's fair to say that the gentle, emotional nature of the Moon does not flourish under the cold, hard glare of Saturn. This is the classic insecurity aspect. It is very hard to feel truly good about oneself and so painful relationships that mirror the lack of self-worth are often attracted. At least, this will be the case until inner confidence is found.

On a purely physical level, Saturn constricts the natural flow of the Moon, so for women with this aspect menstrual and reproductive difficulties can ensue and fertility can be low or absent. This, however, is a reflection of the lack of inner fertility or creativity but, by becoming more full on the inside and not needing a partner or a baby to bring fulfilment, miracles can happen.

Many of the problems associated with this aspect are a result of emotional coldness and inhibition. It is very hard for people with Saturn imposing on their Moon to express their feelings openly and demonstratively. Such a repression or blockage of emotion understandably leads to physical problems. People with this aspect really need to work on their levels of self-esteem so that they feel more deserving of the good things, and so that they become confident enough to start expressing their emotions. If this doesn't happen, depression, anxiety and fear are likely to dominate.

HERBS AND SPICES: damiana, dong quai root, false unicorn, fennel, motherwort

BACH FLOWERS: chestnut bud, chicory, gentian, gorse, honeysuckle, larch, mustard, pine, rock rose, rock water, walnut, wild rose

COLOURS: orange, yellow

AROMATHERAPY OILS: geranium, jasmine, melissa, rose, ylang ylang

VITAMINS AND MINERALS: folic acid, vitamin E

Moon–Uranus

KEYWORDS: Emotional instability

When the quirky, erratic Uranus meets the emotional Moon the result can be somewhat irrational. The emotional state is unlikely to be calm and centred for very long, unless a practice such as meditation or yoga is regularly performed. Emotionally speaking, these people don't know whether they're coming or going and anxiety, panic attacks and phobias may well be the result. For women, the menstrual cycle may be haphazard, so relying on the calendar method of contraception may not be advisable, as fertility could occur outside the normal time.

If you have this aspect in your chart, you need to ground yourself and ensure that you receive regular periods of calm and relaxation, otherwise your overly excitable nature could result in breakdowns in health and a stressed-out nervous system.

HERBS AND SPICES: angelica root, chamomile, fennel, motherwort, skullcap, valerian

BACH FLOWERS: cherry plum, impatiens, rescue remedy, rock rose, star of Bethlehem, walnut

COLOURS: brown, green, pink, rust, turquoise

AROMATHERAPY OILS: chamomile, frankincense, melissa, neroli, patchouli, rose

VITAMINS AND MINERALS: magnesium, manganese, vitamin B complex

Moon–Neptune

KEYWORDS: The emotional sponge

Here Neptune breaks down any sense of emotional separateness and the resulting desire to connect with all and sundry can lead to dependency on drugs or alcohol. Water retention is a common problem with this aspect, from premenstrual bloating to swelling of the ankles. Any problem involving fluids is likely to be emotional in origin. Swellings are perhaps a sign of being too impressionable and taking in too much – absorbing other people's emotions may be very saintly but it doesn't do much for your health.

With this aspect, stronger boundaries need to be erected – try visualising a protective bubble of white light around yourself to prevent unwanted thoughts and emotions permeating your aura.

A fighting spirit may be absent, which lessens the effectiveness of your immune system. Try using your powerful imagination to visualise your immune system fighting off invaders.

HERBS AND SPICES: echinacea, garlic, goldenseal

BACH FLOWERS: centaury, clematis, honeysuckle, pine, scleranthus

COLOURS: orange, purple, red, turquoise

AROMATHERAPY OILS: cypress, geranium, juniper, lavender, rosemary

VITAMINS AND MINERALS: potassium, selenium, sodium, vitamins A, C, E, zinc

Moon–Pluto

KEYWORD: Suppression

The biggest danger to health with this aspect is emotional suppression. When Pluto aspects the Moon the emotional nature is intensified, but if the aspect is a hard one, these emotions are likely to be blocked. This is the equivalent of the little Dutch boy sticking his finger in the dyke – sooner or later there's going to be an enormous deluge. The trouble with this aspect is that emotional hurts can linger for an awfully long time and several hurts can cause a build-up of painful emotional suppression that is kept buried due to the fear of experiencing and releasing these feelings. But this is what must happen to ensure the health and happiness of these people.

Physically, Moon–Pluto aspects are associated with female reproductive problems such as heavy or difficult periods, womb problems, ovarian cysts and fibroids. These are largely reflective of concerns around being a woman or a mother, and may be linked to issues regarding one's own mother.

The colon and bowel can also be weakened with this aspect and any problems here such as IBS, constipation and digestive cramps are a reflection that on a psychological or emotional level we are afraid to let go. Many people with this aspect have a fear of abandonment or loss, so clinging and holding on becomes a way of attempting to alleviate the fear.

Stomach problems may also be linked to this aspect as the destructiveness of Pluto strikes fear into the heart of the lunar need for security. However, because emotional security is fundamental to our well-being, the intensity and insecurity of this aspect can bring about a whole range of physical problems.

Developing inner security is the key to dealing with this aspect.

HERBS AND SPICES: aloe vera, cascara sagrada, dong quai root, raspberry leaf, yarrow

BACH FLOWERS: chestnut bud, chicory, gorse, holly, honeysuckle, mustard, red chestnut, sweet chestnut, walnut, willow

COLOURS: pink, white

AROMATHERAPY OILS: chamomile, cypress, jasmine, melissa, rose

VITAMINS AND MINERALS: iron, selenium, vitamin E, zinc

PHILOSOPHY: letting go of the past

5

Mercury –
Your State of Mind

*'We don't see things as they are,
we see things as we are.'*
ANAÏS NIN

Mercury is the messenger, the gatherer and exchanger of information. In Greek mythology it was the link between humans and the gods and was renowned for its mischievous nature. Mercury is dual-natured, always having one face in the light and one in the shadows, and this has led to the schizophrenic or split personality that is associated with Mercury and its sign, Gemini. Mercury certainly is changeable and can adapt to any person or situation, but the danger lies in it not being sure who it is, as it can be all things to all people.

The doors of perception

One of the important things to remember about Mercury is that it has a chameleon and androgynous nature – in other words, it is neutral on its own and in the chart takes on the colour of any planet that aspects it. This can therefore lead to a subjective way of viewing the world, which is how the vast majority of us operates – our thoughts, opinions and perceptions are based on our previous experiences, which may not be a true representation of what is actually happening. Imagine that Mercury is conjunct Jupiter – our perceptions and thoughts will be exaggerated and combined with great optimism, while with Neptune things become idealised and distorted, vague and confused. And with Saturn, we will tend to see things more negatively than they really are. This has important implications for all of us because it enables us to understand that our view of reality will be different to that of our neighbours, our parents, our friends and our partners. And once we realise that everyone is operating with a slightly different reality, we can be more tolerant of ourselves and others. Not only that, but having realised that there are more realities than ours, we can change the one we have if we don't like it by changing the way we think.

Physiological correspondences

Astrologically, Mercury rules the respiratory system – the throat, lungs and trachea – and it has a bearing on our hands and speech and hearing. Our mental well-being or lack of it is revealed by Mercury. It also has an influence on our nervous system, but since this is more the domain of Uranus we will look at it in a later chapter.

The respiratory system

Breathing is a Mercurial function as it is an exchange of sorts – converting oxygen to carbon dioxide – and is carried out by the nervous system. Air is what links us all together; we all breathe the same air, and so respiratory problems such as asthma can have their psychological roots in sharing, giving and receiving. Because asthmatics cannot let go of the out breath, there is often an underlying fear or panic of there not being enough, so holding on becomes an issue. Ultimately asthma is about trusting and letting go.

Issues of independence are also stored in the lungs, as our first breath reflects our separation from our mother. Too much smothering or, conversely, having to shoulder everything on our own can lead to problems with lungs and breathing. Unexpressed sadness and grief can lead to lung disorders, as can a suppressed desire to express ourselves. The out breath enables us to speak (try talking while breathing in), so asthma in particular can be reflective of long-held sadness and grief, or wanting to express ourselves in some way – creatively, emotionally or verbally – but feeling unable to do so.

The mental processes

Mercury – the planet of the mind – governs our mental processes, the way we think and express ourselves. The sign, house placement and aspects to Mercury will determine how we view the world and what beliefs we hold. It will reveal whether we are an optimist or a pessimist, and naïve and trusting like a child or a hard-edged cynic. Mercury is therefore psychological in essence and a healthy Mercury is essential for our mental well-being. Understanding how our mind works is absolutely crucial for us because it is the mind that controls our day-to-day lives and determines our actions. For example, if we get a bill that is far higher than normal, it is our mind that decides our emotional reaction. We'll either panic and get in a flap (Uranus), get depressed and fearful (Saturn), refuse to face up to it and have another drink (Neptune), or think optimistically that an error has occurred and a quick phone call will sort out the problem (Jupiter).

The way in which our mind works will determine the way we perceive a situation, which then determines how we react emotionally. A negative psychological pattern will therefore create negative emotions whenever that pattern is triggered. We always have a choice of how to perceive an event – we can get depressed because we've had five days of rain and grey skies, or we can see the rain as supplying our water and feeding the earth. Taking the latter perception, suddenly a rainy day can be a cause for happiness and gratitude.

Negative mental states

Consider the following negative mental states and identify yours: suspicion, doubt, fear, cynicism, depression, criticism, pessimism, paranoia, worry, prudishness, judging, control, complaining.

In many cases we display one of those tendencies in only one area of our lives, and therefore we may not generally associate ourselves with it. For example, someone may be pessimistic when it comes to money, believing that he or she will never win anything, or that as soon as some comes in something will arise to make sure it goes straight back out again. But in all other areas of life this person could be an optimist and see him or herself as such. So go through each area of your life (health, relationships, money, work/career, family, body image, self-worth etc.) and see which areas are most prone to negative perceptions. You can be sure that this is where your Mercury will be afflicted in some way.

Living in harmony with Mercury – self-expression and a peaceful mind

Because we live in a very Mercurial society – fast-paced and communicative – we could suppose that we are all living in harmony with our Mercurys. Actually, the pendulum has swung too far, with our lives being too busy, and so we are seeing the negative aspects of Mercury – irritability, depression, nervous tension and stress. Asthma (a Mercurial disease) is increasing rapidly, and 40 million people worldwide are on Prozac – that's a lot of unhappy people out there. Instead of looking at short cuts and quick fixes (very Mercurial) we need to be looking at ways in which we can simultaneously calm down the Mercurial aspect of life while looking at what it really needs.

Self-expression

Because Mercury is the planet of speech, this is where we will find our ability to express ourselves. As independent beings, it is vital that we feel we have a voice, that we are heard and that we count for something. Those people who have a weak or suppressed Mercury may feel frustrated at not being able to express themselves in the way they'd like. This can then turn to anger and resentment as their true self isn't being expressed. This can manifest in a number of ways, from not being able to speak up in groups or not having the confidence to ask for what we want, to not having the confidence to express ourselves creatively or feeling undervalued in our work. Perhaps our job doesn't allow us to express ourselves – if so we need to look at ways of changing that or, if that's not possible, changing our job. If we really want to draw, sing, write, dance or paint, but have always held back through fear or lack of confidence, we need to take the plunge, otherwise we will remain frustrated.

Reducing over-stimulation

Mercury is essentially about communication, but not the sort of frantic communication we are subjected to now through mobile phones, text messages, email, fax, radio, television, the internet, 24-hour news coverage and the media. In short we are being over-stimulated. We are constantly bombarded with images and messages from the media, but not the sort that feed our soul. To be truly communicating, we should be expressing ourselves in a way that reflects who we really are. Mercury in an air sign, for example, would be good at expressing ideas or knowledge, perhaps as a writer, teacher or speaker. Word games such as Scrabble or crosswords would keep the mind healthy, as would reading. Mercury in a water sign, however, would be ideally suited to the expression of feelings through an artistic means or through some caring role. In an earth sign, Mercury would function best through a practical expression – either through ideas that can have a physical or tangible benefit for people or in creative ways such as pottery, gardening or craft work. Mercury in a fire sign needs to be producing ambitious ideas and either acting on them or getting other people to act on them.

Discovering what our individual Mercury needs and fulfilling those needs will go a long way to keeping ourselves mentally stable.

Intrusion

Because of the intense communicative nature of the society in which we now live, it is virtually impossible to get away from noise. We have become accustomed to it, and as a result many of us now feel uncomfortable with silence. We must have the television or radio on if there's no one else for company. Our addiction to mobile phones means that others have constant access to us – we don't have any time or space that's truly our own, and this can be very detrimental to our mental well-being. It is therefore vital that we allow for some quiet time in our daily lives, if only to recapture a sense of peace.

Your Mercury is out of balance when:

- O You're addicted to your mobile phone, television, radio or computer

- O You can't remember the last time you had a quiet moment

- O You find silence uncomfortable

- O You're regularly forgetful or confused

- O You're often nervous, jumpy or irritable

- O You find it difficult to switch off your mind or mental chatter

- O You suffer from insomnia

- O You're on antidepressants or feel down a lot of the time

To increase the strength of your Mercury and psychological well-being:

○ Take regular time out from the hectic world; create a space for 20 minutes a day that's yours and yours alone

○ Have one day a week at least when you avoid newspapers, magazines, television and other media avenues that try to form your opinions for you – whose mind is it anyway?

○ Practise meditation, yoga or tai-chi to calm your mind down

○ Don't be a slave to your phone – just because it's ringing doesn't necessarily mean you have to answer it, especially if you're in the middle of relaxing

○ Don't take your mobile phone on holiday

○ Practise a physical or creative pursuit that takes you out of your head – gardening, cooking, walking, sports, pottery, painting etc.

○ Develop your imagination, instead of letting the television do it for you: play a game, write a short story, play an instrument, listen to music, paint a picture, read a fictional book

○ Write a journal or keep a dream diary so you can learn to understand what your subconscious is trying to tell you

○ Spend some time in nature: the tranquillity of the natural world can be very restorative for frantic minds

Aspects to Mercury (including transits)

Mercury–Sun

See page 32.

Mercury–Moon

See page 43.

Mercury–Venus

KEYWORD: Diplomacy

Because Mercury and Venus are never very far apart, the only aspects they can form are conjunction, semi-sextile and the sextile, therefore they don't have much bearing on health, and the endocrine glands are the main function of Mercury–Venus.

Mercury–Mars

KEYWORDS: Fast forward

This is an excitable aspect that can lead to irritability and nervousness. This 'jumpiness' then translates itself on a physical level through nervous tics and twitches, spasms and inflammation of nervous tissue. The most troubling by-product of this aspect can be an overactive mind. The head may be full of thoughts – angry, critical, impatient or judgmental ones being the most probable.

However, this aspect isn't deemed to be particularly threatening to health, and the worst elements of this combination can be reduced by incorporating periods of relaxation into the day. Meditation would be especially beneficial.

HERBS AND SPICES: aloe vera, chamomile, skullcap, valerian

BACH FLOWERS: beech, heather, holly, impatiens, vervain, vine

COLOURS: pastel green, pastel pink, turquoise

AROMATHERAPY OILS: chamomile, cypress, lavender, marjoram, neroli, rose, sandalwood

VITAMINS AND MINERALS: magnesium, manganese, vitamin B complex

IDEAL THERAPY: meditation

Mercury–Jupiter

KEYWORDS: The big thinker

Jupiter is the planet of exaggeration, so when it is combined with the planet governing the mind things can be blown out of all proportion. Over-stimulation is the main problem here. On the positive side, this combination can also give great optimism and hope, both productive traits in the creation and maintenance of good health. If you have a hard aspect between these two planets, it is best to cut down or avoid the use of any stimulants – especially caffeine (coffee, tea, cola and chocolate) and nicotine. Artificial additives such as sweeteners, colourings, preservatives and flavourings are also best avoided as they all have an irritating effect on the nervous system and liver.

HERBS AND SPICES: dandelion root, milkthistle

BACH FLOWERS: agrimony, beech, heather, impatiens, water violet

COLOURS: green, turquoise, yellow

AROMATHERAPY OILS: frankincense, neroli, rosewood, sandalwood

VITAMINS AND MINERALS: biotin, chromium, vitamin B complex

Mercury–Saturn

KEYWORDS: The serious thinker

The main problem with this aspect is mental heaviness that manifests itself on a psychological level with a tendency towards a cynical or melancholy mood that expects the worst, or even depression. There is a large amount of fear when these two planets get together, mainly because Saturn infuses the mind with a certain greyness and a lack of confidence in one's own talents and abilities – especially those of a mental nature such as studying. This inadequacy may be compounded by an actual tendency towards slowness in picking things up. Therefore children with this aspect need extra encouragement as they may take longer to learn than their peers.

There may also be an inclination towards negative beliefs and criticism, which in turn can lead to arthritis and other bone and joint problems.

HERBS AND SPICES: basil, ginger, motherwort, St John's wort

BACH FLOWERS: aspen, beech, cherry plum, chestnut bud, gentian, hornbeam, mimulus, mustard, pine, red chestnut, rock water, water violet, white chestnut, willow

COLOURS: orange, pink, yellow

AROMATHERAPY OILS: bergamot, jasmine, neroli, orange, rosemary, vetivert

VITAMINS AND MINERALS: folic acid, potassium

Mercury–Uranus

KEYWORDS: The higher mind

When the two planets governing the mind get together the results can be electrifying. On the upside, those with this aspect may have genius potential, but on the downside, they may have difficulty switching their brains off, which can lead to mental overload, nervous tension, stress, irritability, impatience and mental instability. People with this aspect may sometimes feel like they're going crazy, or that if others could see into their minds they'd be certified. The best way to alleviate this aspect is to calm the mind down on a regular basis, therefore meditation is ideal.

On a physical level this mental hyperactivity, if not curbed, can result in accidents, as the person is always in a rush and is too erratic or scattered in his or her thinking to focus correctly on what they're doing. It can result in all manner of nervous habits that aren't usually a threat to health itself but can be unsettling.

HERBS AND SPICES: angelica root, chamomile, skullcap, valerian

BACH FLOWERS: cherry plum, impatiens, rescue remedy, rock rose, scleranthus, star of Bethlehem, vervain, water violet

COLOURS: burgundy, green, pink, turquoise

AROMATHERAPY OILS: chamomile, frankincense, lavender, melissa, neroli, patchouli, sandalwood

VITAMINS AND MINERALS: magnesium, manganese, vitamin B complex

Mercury–Neptune

KEYWORDS: Colourful imagination

The main problems with this aspect are psychological as Neptune undermines the mind's ability to function correctly, leading to confusion, fears, fainting, hallucinations and, at worst, nervous breakdowns. An overactive imagination can be used to create irrational fears and phobias, or it can be used constructively in the form of visualisation, guided imagery and meditation. People with this aspect need to find an artistic or spiritual means of communication; painting, photography, prayer or music would be ideal.

HERBS AND SPICES: motherwort, valerian, vervain

BACH FLOWERS: agrimony, aspen, centaury, cerato, cherry plum, clematis, gentian, hornbeam, scleranthus, wild oat, wild rose

COLOURS: orange, purple, yellow

AROMATHERAPY OILS: basil, chamomile, frankincense, lavender, melissa, sandalwood

VITAMINS AND MINERALS: potassium, vitamin B complex

Mercury–Pluto

KEYWORDS: Knowledge is power

Pluto can have a most disturbing effect on the psyche. It symbolises the underworld, and so when these two planets meet the effect can be quite dark and depressing. Pluto imbues the mental processes with enormous powers of perception – these people can just 'know' things without being told, and it's this powerful ability to probe their own depths and the depths of others that can lead them to be brilliant psychologists, psychotherapists and counsellors. However, if not channelled constructively, the suspicion, fear and paranoia of Pluto can lead to all sorts of mental problems, culminating in mental exhaustion and a fear of insanity. With this aspect the mind can descend into darkness, creating obsessive thoughts, paranoia, compulsions and great fears. The only way to overcome this is to go into the fear instead of trying to block or control it. When we face our fears and embrace them in love, they dissolve into nothing.

On a physical level, it relates to the breaking down and regeneration of nervous tissue.

HERBS AND SPICES: motherwort, sage leaves, St John's wort, valerian, vervain

BACH FLOWERS: aspen, beech, cherry plum, crab apple, holly, red chestnut, rock rose, sweet chestnut, vine, white chestnut

COLOURS: orange, white, yellow

AROMATHERAPY OILS: bergamot, jasmine, melissa, orange, rose, thyme

VITAMINS AND MINERALS: vitamin B complex

6

Venus –
The Art of Love

*'The supreme happiness of life is the conviction
that we are loved.'*
Victor Hugo

Since Venus is famous for being the planet of love and beauty and all things lovely
we may think her influence upon our health and well-being is automatically
benevolent. But appearances can be deceptive, never more so than where the
beautiful outward appearance of Venus is concerned. While it's true that many of
her interactions with the other planets are largely benign, if her needs are ignored
her effect upon health can be quite brutal. This is largely because she governs love
and pleasure, and if we don't receive enough love we quickly wither and die. Since
sensual pleasure and the feel-good factor are also her domain, Venus can show
where we get our pleasure and what we need to feel good. Because of this, she is
emotional in nature. If we have a weak or adversely aspected Venus, it may then be
difficult for us to feel good about very much – including ourselves.

Mostly though, Venus reveals how we are in relationships and how we like to
give and receive love. You don't have to be a psychologist to see how unhappy
relationships can have an adverse effect on our inner levels of peace and well-
being. Let's take a deeper look at the function of relationships.

'Mirror mirror on the wall, who is the fairest of them all?'

Next time you see a beautiful hand-held antique mirror think of Venus, for the mirror is closely linked to her symbol. Venus allows us to see ourselves through our relationships, as clearly as if reflected in a mirror. This is rarely a conscious process, but over time we come to learn an awful lot about ourselves through our relations with others – particularly our intimate relationships. Here we see our hidden potential as mirrored by the traits in those we really admire, and our denied shadows, revealed by the traits that press our buttons and make us upset, irritable or angry.

A strong or well-placed Venus will indicate someone for whom relationships are very important, whereas a difficult Venus will show low self-worth reflected through difficult relationships and the lessons we need to learn with regard to these relationships.

Physiological correspondences

Venus is the regulator of the planetary system and strives to keep a balance in all things – including our bodies. Her function within the body is to balance and regulate, therefore her domains are the kidneys, the bladder, homeostasis, hormonal function and the ovaries.

The kidneys

Since the primary function of Venus is to balance and regulate, we are right to expect the kidneys to come under her domain. The kidneys' role within the body is to create balance and equilibrium. They extract unwanted substances from the blood and perform a delicate acid–alkaline balancing act. This balancing of opposites – night and day, male and female, ying and yang – is symbolic of how we relate with our opposites – namely in our intimate relationships or marriage. It is therefore probable that any problem with our kidneys is reflecting an imbalance within our relationships. If our relationships are unbalanced in any way, if we carry around fears to do with the relationship such as emotional insecurity, or if we harbour unexpressed anger, guilt, sadness or grief in relation to our partner or a past partner, we may experience kidney difficulties. It's important then that we are true to ourselves in the area of relationships and we must take care to ensure that we have balance and equality within them.

The bladder

When the kidneys have successfully filtered out the impurities, they are expelled by the body via the urine. Urine – liquid waste matter – represents our negative emotions. Bladder problems such as cystitis are often revealing a state of hanging on to negative feelings – hence the expression 'being pissed off'. It may be that we're angry and fed up or we can't move on emotionally, finding it difficult or painful to let go of negative feelings. Many incidences of cystitis are linked to relationship changes or problems. Maybe we have a fear of intimacy, especially if it's a new relationship (honeymoon cystitis), or if a relationship has come to an end we may find it difficult to let go and move on. Whatever the specific cause, all cystitis cases are requiring us to let go. When we consider that love doesn't seek to possess or hold on, it seems fitting that Venus – the planet of love – would create this ailment to show us that maybe we need to be more loving.

Hormones

Various organs in the body such as the pancreas release hormones or chemicals. Under hormonal function come the thyroid gland, the pituitary gland and the adrenal glands.

The adrenal glands are situated on the kidneys (thus linking kidney disorders to fear) and serve a most essential purpose – when we are frightened they release the adrenaline we need to cope with a difficult or frightening situation. However, because of the highly stressful conditions under which we all now live, our adrenals release far more adrenaline than might be good for us, which has a potentially very damaging effect on our bodies. Every fearful or anxious thought or feeling that we have has a chemical effect on the body. It therefore makes sense to try and avoid focusing on fears and doubts about the future, because such fearful focusing can have as great a negative physical response as an actual dangerous situation. The antidote to fear is love, so by bringing the main Venusian state of being into the equation, we can re-create balance in these Venusian areas.

Living in harmony with Venus – love, harmony and beauty

It is important to remember that any symptoms that are Venusian in nature can be relieved by being more loving or balanced. Love is the keyword with Venus and she probably has a far greater effect on our health than we realise. If we consider that babies can actually die if deprived of love for long, it becomes clear that no living thing – humans, animals, even plants – can thrive in a loveless atmosphere. To test this out, consider a time when you felt truly loved compared to a time when you were heartbroken, let down or deceived by a loved one.

Our ability to express love and affection is vital for our well-being. If our heart is frozen due to painful experiences in the past, our loving energy cannot flow and the resulting block can create physical symptoms. When we do things for others from our hearts and out of love and compassion, we are taken out of ourselves, which frees us from narcissistic tendencies and an unhealthy dwelling on our own issues and problems. The more we focus on our own failings in a lamenting 'poor me' style, the greater the downward spiral. Venus reminds us that genuinely loving others is a wonderful way to alleviate many of our own problems.

Self-love

While it is important to be loving to others, we perhaps don't realise that it's just as important to be loving towards ourselves. The keyword here is balance and it's a very fine line between being selfish and healthy consideration of our own needs. Many of the above physical conditions result from a lack of self-love. If we don't value ourselves, we create feelings of worthlessness, shame and guilt – classic breeding grounds for ill-health. What Venus is asking of us is a perfect balance between self-love and love for others. When we can love and respect ourselves as much as we do our partners, children, parents and friends, we'll not only be happier and healthier but we'll have more satisfying relationships, because people have a tendency to mirror back to us our own feeling of worth, or lack of it. If we don't value ourselves very much, we'll attract a partner who puts us down and increases our feelings of worthlessness.

Relating

Our relationships give us our emotional nourishment and are absolutely crucial to our well-being. They can be a real source of joy, but can also be the bane of our lives. Relationship problems usually occur due to misunderstandings and poor communication. Perception is the key here: how we perceive an incident may be completely different to how our partner perceives it, and this may then create confusion or hurt. It's a similar scenario with the giving and receiving of love: we may not actually realise that our partner loves us, simply because he or she doesn't do the things for us that we do for them. For example, your partner may be a practical lover, showing love through providing security such as paying the mortgage and putting food on the table, whereas you might express love through physical affection and words.

Wherever Venus is found in our charts, it will reveal where we are most loving and – equally – where we are most capable of attracting love. Venus in Aries has a completely different way of expressing love than someone with Venus in Virgo. The former may show love through warm enthusiastic and passionate actions, whereas Virgo would be more subtle, showing love through caring, dutiful acts. This simple knowledge can help us understand why our partners demonstrate their love in a different way from us, and why that can result in confusion and upset.

Of course, relating isn't just about our intimate relationship with our significant other. It also extends to our friends and acquaintances. How well we get on with others determines how happy we are on a day-to-day basis. If we constantly find ourselves arguing or disagreeing with others, we will find it hard to have a natural *joie de vivre*. Conversely, if our relations with others are harmonious, then even the briefest encounter with the assistant in the corner shop can be a source of joy.

Beauty and art

As humans, we tend to be drawn to the beautiful, whether it be embodied in a person, a natural scene or a painting or sculpture. Although a strongly placed Venus – such as in Libra or Taurus or conjunct the Sun, or planets in the Venus-ruled Libra or Taurus – will create a deeper need for beauty, we all respond to that which is pleasing to the eye. Of course beauty need not conform to obvious or clichéed images such as a perfect face or a sleek sports car – we might find beauty in all kinds of things, and the more we look for it the more we will find it.

Art also comes under the domain of Venus, for the purpose of art is to uplift and stimulate or please the senses. If you don't already know, take a moment to consider what you consider to be a work of art. It could come under the traditional umbrella of art in the form of painting or sculpture, but it may be a beautifully presented meal, a dream garden or a pleasantly arranged bouquet of flowers that does it for you. Take time to become aware of what makes you feel good inside and make an effort to spend more time being surrounded by your work of art, or if you have any creative abilities you could create your own masterpieces.

Your Venus is out of balance when:

O You overindulge in the pleasure of the day, whether it be food, chocolate, drugs, sex or alcohol

O You're a relationship junkie, lurching from one to another, each time thinking 'this is the one'

O Your day revolves around the hairdresser's, beauty salons and shopping

O You can't live without your little luxuries

O Your desire for the finer things in life overrides your ethics – e.g. you drive a petrol guzzler, or use products that involve cruelty to animals

O You have had or would contemplate cosmetic surgery

O You're addicted to shopping, particularly clothes, beauty products and luxury items

To increase the strength of your Venus and the health of your kidneys:

O Learn to like yourself: make a list of all your good points, talents and abilities

O Strive for balance and moderation in all things

O Are your relationships based on equality? If not, look at ways in which you can redress the balance.

O How much beauty is there in your life? Maybe you don't need to actually do anything other than notice the beauty that already surrounds you – a child's smile, your lover's eyes, the dew on the grass.

O Create more harmony in your home: practise the art of feng shui; throw out your clutter and decorate your home in harmonious colours and fabrics

O Become more appreciative of what you have: start a gratitude journal and write down five things you are thankful for at the end of each day

○ Stimulate your senses: have a regular aromatherapy massage, experiment with new foods and introduce new scents into your home

○ A candlelit aromatic bath is the ultimate Venus experience. For sheer luxurious indulgence, why not savour a couple of your favourite chocolates or enjoy a glass of your favourite tipple at the same time? But remember that moderation is the key.

○ Create more beautiful relationships – refuse to be drawn into petty arguments

○ Are you happy with your social life? Do you have a wide enough variety of supportive friends and enjoyable experiences to look forward to? If not, be the one to start the ball rolling. Invite some friends round for supper or organise an outing to see a play. A good social life helps create inner radiance.

○ Develop your people skills. Be determined to find something good in even the most awkward of people. By focusing on the good points in others, we alleviate the destructive need to criticise – and win ourselves more friends and admirers too.

Aspects to Venus (including transits)

Venus–Sun
See page 32.

Venus–Moon
See page 43.

Venus–Mercury
See page 55.

Venus–Mars

KEYWORDS: The archetypal opposites

'Men are from Mars, Women are from Venus': how quickly this quotation became widespread as an encapsulation of the differences between the sexes. While there are certain differences, they're never more exaggerated or obvious than in relationships of people with Venus–Mars aspects because these planets symbolise opposites. The main problem with a Venus–Mars hard aspect is one of anger or irritation toward the partner or members of the opposite sex in general – largely due to feelings of being misunderstood. If this anger is repressed, the result is resentment and over time this can lead to cystitis or kidney infections. An infection in physical terms is a battle – the white blood cells rise up against an invader. It's not surprising, then, that infections are usually symbolic of anger at someone, so if we are prone to infections we need to be honest about who or what we're angry about. Cystitis or a kidney infection will more often than not point towards the marriage or long-term partner.

HERBS AND SPICES: cleavers, cornsilk, horsetail, juniper, parsley, thyme

BACH FLOWERS: beech, holly, impatiens

COLOURS: blue, pink, white

AROMATHERAPY OILS: benzoin, cedarwood, fennel, geranium, parsley, rose, ylang ylang

VITAMINS AND MINERALS: phosphorus, potassium, vitamin C, zinc

Venus–Jupiter

KEYWORDS: The pleasure seeker

The biggest problem we have with Venus and Jupiter is one of excess and over-indulgence. Even the hard aspects between these two planets do little to disturb the psychological or emotional well-being of the person, other than to create a love of the good life and excessive feelings of entitlement that can result in greed and unrestrained behaviour. A love of sweet and rich foods can be the biggest problem here, which can put a tremendous strain on the liver. There may also be excessive glandular secretions and a reluctance to exercise. Obviously a sugary or high-fat diet combined with a lack of exercise and a lazy approach will not do wonders for the body, and therefore anyone with these aspects needs to make a serious effort towards discipline and self-restraint.

HERBS AND SPICES: burdock, dandelion root, milkthistle

BACH FLOWER: heather

COLOURS: cream, turquoise, white, yellow

AROMATHERAPY OILS: eucalyptus, pine

VITAMINS AND MINERALS: biotin, chromium

IDEAL THERAPY: exercise!

Venus–Saturn

KEYWORDS: Relationship insecurity

A Venus–Saturn aspect can be one of the most problematic, largely because the two energies embodied in these planets are virtual opposites. Venus represents not only how we feel about ourselves but also the good things in life such as money, a loving relationship and health, and how entitled we feel we are to receive them. Saturn is a restricting and limiting force on such things, so consequently when Saturn meets Venus the result is often one of low self-worth coupled with feelings of insecurity and lack of entitlement. The loving warmth and contentment of Venus is frustrated by the cold limiting energy of Saturn and so there is frequently a lack of joviality and inner happiness.

Not surprisingly, all this inner discontent can have serious repercussions on health. Women may suffer from hormonal disorders that can result in problems with the ovaries (especially polycystic), while kidney stones may be indicative of relationship fears. Feelings of being unloved and rejected may lead to depression. Women with this aspect may be sexually inhibited and need to become more relaxed with their bodies and their femininity, while men with this aspect may have difficulty relating to women and thus forming fulfilling relationships.

HERBS AND SPICES: cleavers, dong quai root (women), fennel, ginseng (men), parsley

BACH FLOWERS: chicory, crab apple, holly, mustard, pine, rock water, willow

COLOURS: orange, pink, red, rose

AROMATHERAPY OILS: melissa, neroli, patchouli, rose, sandalwood, ylang ylang

VITAMINS AND MINERALS: folic acid, iodine, phosphorus, potassium, vitamin E, zinc

Venus–Uranus

KEYWORDS: The freedom seeker

An aspect between romantic Venus and electrifying Uranus can create a lot of spark in relationships, and people born with these aspects do usually need a fair amount of stimulation and excitement in their love lives. What happens when the relationship settles into a more predictable, secure affair, though, could well be cause for concern, because this aspect detests the safe and predictable – at least it does when it comes to love and romance. It is understandable, then, that these aspects have a bad press when it comes to creating successful long-term relationships, as not only is it easy for the individual to become bored, but he or she also needs a lot of freedom. Unfortunately, this can give the partner the message that he or she isn't really needed – and who wouldn't eventually tire of such a cool, unresponsive approach and look for someone more capable of supplying a loving warmth and closeness? What's really going on here, then, is a psychological fear of rejection and at the same time a fear of commitment. This all translates itself on a physical level through the sex drive, which can be spasmodic, and a general instability in the hormonal system. When the person can be more constant when relating to others, his or her hormones may settle down too. Spasmodic kidney pains are also reflective of erratic relations with others.

The key to dealing with this aspect is to be less selfish in relationships and to develop more consistency, warmth and closeness with others. To give love freely in a committed relationship is the ultimate aim for people with this aspect.

HERBS AND SPICES: chamomile, fennel, parsley, valerian

BACH FLOWERS: heather, water violet

COLOURS: blue, pink

AROMATHERAPY OILS: chamomile, geranium, melissa, rose

VITAMINS AND MINERALS: iodine, magnesium, manganese

Venus–Neptune

KEYWORD: Idealism

Aspects between the two planets governing art, beauty and idealism can have a wonderfully uplifting effect – especially if the individual is at all artistically minded. However, problems can arise in relationships as the idealism of Neptune propels the individual to continuously search for the perfect relationship. This means that a great deal of disillusionment can arise with people who have Venus–Neptune aspects, because their love lives rarely measure up to their ideal. They may live more in a fantasy world than in real life, and the true, committed and intimate relationship that is the bedrock of good health and happiness can forever elude them.

On a physical level then, these aspects can translate themselves as kidney problems and poor glandular function, with more hormones being released than is required. The pancreas may also need to be protected. Because this aspect creates a certain weakness and reluctance to face reality, people with these aspects are prone to escapism – especially through food, sex, romance, drink or drugs.

The key to dealing with this aspect is to incorporate some realism into life. Instead of seeking the ideal fantasy man or woman, learn to look instead for the beauty that exists in the current partner and work at developing closeness and intimacy with him or her. Realise, also, that escaping through drink or drugs will not alleviate any problems, only postpone them and make them worse in the long run.

HERBS AND SPICES: cascara sagrada, comfrey, evening primrose, liquorice

BACH FLOWER: clematis

COLOUR: green

AROMATHERAPY OILS: chamomile, geranium, juniper, lavender

VITAMINS AND MINERALS: iodine, phosphorus, potassium

Venus–Pluto

KEYWORD: Seduction

When the beautiful Venus is imbued with the dark, powerful essence of Pluto, the result is a seductive, emotionally intense and potentially lethal cocktail. Anyone brave enough to take a sip may well come back for more, yet end up regretting it. The purpose of such an aspect is to experience fully all the highs and lows of relationships, both emotionally and sexually. There may be some wonderfully high points, but some desperately low ones too. The Venus–Pluto person wouldn't want it any other way, for extremes in love is what he or she subconsciously seeks. However, uncontrolled passionate impulses can lead to problems, as can the suppression or denial of the individual's intensely passionate nature. Obviously a balance is needed between suppression and all-out excess. If such a balance isn't found, this may eventually lead to physical problems in the kidneys and reproductive areas. These are symbolic of imbalances in relationships or shame regarding excess or suppression of the powerful sex drive. To transform this potentially destructive aspect, there first needs to be an acceptance of the self and the shadow side with all its sexual hang-ups or deviancies, and then a willingness to control and channel the passions into a loving relationship or creative outlet.

HERBS AND SPICES: aloe vera, damiana, dong quai root, saw palmetto berries

BACH FLOWERS: chicory, crab apple, holly

COLOURS: pink, white

AROMATHERAPY OILS: chamomile, cypress, geranium, melissa

VITAMINS AND MINERALS: phosphorus, potassium, selenium, vitamin E

7

Mars – Your Passion for Life

'Fortune has no power over courage.'
LUDOVICO ARIOSTO

Mars, the God of war, represents all that at first glance appears to be detrimental to our well-being and relations with others. With its associations with selfishness, anger, aggression, lust, fights and animalistic responses, Mars has a pretty bad press and its characteristics are ones we are encouraged to rise above, repress or ignore. Surely if we're more like Venus – all charm and loving and forgiving – then we'll be happier and healthier? Well, yes, if we could genuinely be a paragon of virtue, but we wouldn't be human if we didn't get angry from time to time, and anger is the one emotion that we need to be able to express and release if we want to maintain good health. Those who seethe with anger or resentment, while covering it up with smiles and offers to help through gritted teeth, are storing up future problems of quite some magnitude.

Mars and our passion

Mars is one of those planets that's easy to see in a purely negative light. Traditional astrology divides the planets into benefic and malefic, and Mars, being aggressive and selfish, was viewed as malefic. However, every planet has a positive and negative side, and Mars's positive side is its lust for life. Without Mars we'd have no passion or energy to do anything. We'd also be devoid of courage. We'd be apathetic, disinterested folk who never stood up for our rights, or indeed the rights of others. Viewed in this light, Mars enables us to get things done, and a healthy Mars knows the difference between assertiveness and aggression. The fighting spirit associated with Mars provokes us into reacting against whatever we deem to be unfair and, in this sense, is hugely valuable in our society.

A strong Mars that allows the healthy expression of one's own needs, desires and feelings contributes greatly to our state of health. 'Survival of the fittest' is a phrase that can be linked to Martian energy, and astrologically a weak, ineffectual Mars is akin to having a weak, ineffectual immune system, so we need to be very vigilant with our Mars and ensure that it has what it needs to function correctly.

Physiological correspondences

The attacking and defending nature of Mars lends itself well to the body's immunity, fighting off disease and infection. The hot, penetrative element of the planet means that it governs sexual function. Tendons and muscles also come under the jurisdiction of Mars, as does the inflammatory response.

Immune system

Our immune system, consisting of white blood cells, is ever vigilant for invaders and is prepared to go to battle at the first hint of trouble. It is obviously vital to our health as without it we'd be sitting ducks for every virus and infection currently doing the rounds. A strong immune system symbolises our aggression, our ability to fight for our rights and ask for what we want. If we have problems with our immunity, such as regularly going down with colds, flu and other viral complaints or infections that we should be able to overcome, we may need to assess our ability to assert ourselves. In what areas of life are we unable to ask for what we want? Are we suppressing anger and resentment at someone or something? Regularly entertaining infections or inflammations is suggestive of anger and discordant relations. Just as an overactive immune response can do more harm than good by attacking itself (auto-immunity and ME), so we need to be vigilant about being over-aggressive and confrontational, or selfish and disregarding of others.

Perhaps the most obvious and most misunderstood of modern diseases is ME, also known as chronic fatigue syndrome. In the case of ME, Mars is totally absent. The muscles collapse and exhaustion sets in, there is no energy, no will, and no desire. Such weakness is not very well tolerated within our Martian go-getting society. It has taken so long for the medical establishment to acknowledge this disease because it is a physical form of depression (itself a mental anger signature), and the common response to depression is to expect the sufferer to snap out of it. As with depression, ME reveals a lack of purpose and anger turned in on the self. It allows one to give up and be exempt from certain responsibilities such as getting a job or relating with others. It is also common in control freaks who learn the valuable lessons of letting go and delegating, not to mention the humility of accepting they're not the infallible superpeople they think they are. Frequently there is a tendency towards self-obsession, resulting in a strongly egocentric personality, with the person focusing on his or her own problems, trials and tribulations. In other words, ME is often a cry for attention.

Cancer

It is becoming increasingly apparent that certain negative emotions, if repressed over a long period of time, can contribute significantly to one's chances of developing cancer. In the main, it is anger and resentment that are the key emotions, which are symbolic of internalised anger wreaking havoc. The good cells become aggressive, attacking the other cells until the vital organs have been completely destroyed. It is absolutely essential, therefore, that we are aware of any suppressed anger that we may be harbouring.

The difficulty lies in becoming aware of something that has been so successfully denied or hidden away in the basement. A good clue is whether you feel resentful when doing things for others – or for particular individuals. This suggests a state of being in which you feel you ought or should do things, but which in your heart you don't really want to do.

This extends to work as well. Are you in a job that frustrates you, or that isn't what you really want to be doing? Whenever we are being untrue to ourselves, we run the risk of internalising the anger, because we are basically angry with ourselves at feeling unable or afraid to change the situation. To keep ourselves tied to situations that are detrimental to our happiness can create a lot of anger, and the worst cases are when we feel boxed in by lack of choice. Perhaps we feel we can't pursue the job of our dreams because we have a mortgage to pay, or we can't leave an unhappy relationship because our partner won't be able to cope.

These, however, are merely excuses for our own fears, doubts and feelings of guilt. Our Mars wants us to have a go, to meet the challenge, to take the odd risk. Playing it safe all the time, feeling that we have no choices and keeping ourselves limited and restricted is not expressing the energy of Mars.

Another clue to repressed anger is getting regular headaches, migraines, infections and inflammations. These are all physical symptoms of anger. Depression is a mental anger signature, which often results from long-term frustration regarding a lack of purpose or direction.

Perhaps this is why cancer is also linked to retirement. We're no longer of use and have lost our passion for work. This being the case, we need to think very carefully about retirement, and if we do choose to give up our job, we need to find something else that drives us, whether it be paid work or a voluntary activity.

Outward expression

All these symptoms and disorders are a reflection of an out-of-control or underfunctioning Mars. Martian energy was never meant to be internalised – it needs to express itself in challenges, projects, interests and sports or other physical activity. Nor should it be allowed to run riot, so finding a balance between aggression and apathy is essential.

Mars works best in the fire, air and earth signs, and is weakest in the water signs. This is because the energy of Mars in a water sign becomes very emotional and subjective, and is far more likely to be internalised. It's a similar story for Mars in one of the watery houses (4th, 8th and 12th) as here Mars is hidden away and unable to express itself easily. Mars aspected by Saturn makes the expression of Mars very difficult and anger is something likely to be at best very well controlled, and at worst denied altogether.

Living in harmony with Mars – drive, energy and enthusiasm

To express your Martian energy healthily, be clear about what you want and make plans to achieve it. This isn't a green light to ride roughshod over others, which would indicate an uncontrolled and immature Mars, but it is about recognising what you need in order to be happy and fulfilled. Mars is happiest when it has something to do – it quickly becomes frustrated when we drift through life without any sense of purpose. So if you don't already have anything you feel passionate about, find something and use your Mars energy to begin manifesting it. Immunity represents our desire to live: if your immune system is weak and you often get ill, examine why your desire for life is low and consider what you might need to re-ignite the spark.

Being assertive is a symbol of a healthy Mars: being aggressive and argumentative is not. If you frequently find yourself running into disputes with others, engaging in battles or becoming embroiled in arguments, you can be sure your Mars needs taking in hand, otherwise your relationships and general well-being will suffer. If you find yourself on the receiving end of other people's anger, it may be a reflection of your own suppressed anger and lack of assertiveness.

Finding the middle way between doormat and warrior is important to keep your Mars healthy and balanced. Don't be afraid to stand up for what you believe in or for what you want, but at the same time value and acknowledge other people's opinions and needs – even if they differ considerably from your own.

Your Mars is out of balance when:

○ You regularly find yourself involved in arguments or conflict

○ You have angry outbursts or temper tantrums

○ You feel that others aren't listening to you or taking account of your needs

○ You're quick to point out people's faults or complain about services that you perceive as substandard

○ You don't like being wrong

○ You use force or verbal aggression to get your way

○ Your first response to anyone who upsets you is to retaliate

○ You can't stand losing and could be described as competitive

To increase the strength of your Mars and your immunity:

○ Have courage in your convictions: ask for what you want, stand up for your rights and refuse to let others manipulate, bully or abuse you

○ Identify and pursue your passions in life, whether it be through your career or hobbies

○ Acknowledge your more primitive urges such as anger, hate and lust; by accepting them as a part of human nature they lose their power to control you

○ Practise forgiveness – the best and quickest way to release anger and resentment; by understanding that we're all doing the best we can and that all negative actions stem from a place of pain, we can be more tolerant of others

○ Practise diplomacy – you don't have to agree with everything other people say, but you can grant them their right to think, feel and act the way they do

○ If you enjoy sports you have a good outlet for pent-up feelings; if not, find a way to unleash your feelings without hurting others – journal writing, music and dance, painting, martial arts or, as a last resort, pillow bashing!

○ Try to avoid apportioning blame as this only creates conflict

○ Take responsibility for everything that happens in your life. This requires great courage and honesty but if you can accept your part in the negative situations that have occurred throughout your life, much of the blame and anger will disappear.

○ No one is perfect – the realisation that we're all flawed makes it easier to accept people the way they are, and helps us ease up on ourselves too when we fail to live up to certain expectations

Aspects to Mars (including transits)

Mars–Sun

See page 32.

Mars–Moon

See page 44.

Mars–Mercury

See page 55.

Mars–Venus

See page 66.

Mars–Jupiter

KEYWORDS: Courageous arrogance

This is a good aspect for creating health, even with the hard aspects, as the benevolence of Jupiter stimulates the immunity of Mars. It produces a protective influence and people with this aspect should enjoy good health for much of the time. The only danger with this aspect is over-indulgence, arrogance, selfishness and overdoing things with a sense of not knowing one's own limits. These tendencies can then lead to liver problems.

HERBS AND SPICES: burdock, dandelion root, milkthistle

BACH FLOWERS: beech, heather, impatiens, vine, water violet

COLOURS: green, white

AROMATHERAPY OILS: chamomile, eucalyptus, pine

VITAMINS AND MINERALS: biotin, cholin, chromium

Mars–Saturn

KEYWORDS: Controlled repression

Here we run into difficulties – the passionate outward energy of Mars meets the cold, restricting controlled energy of Saturn and creates a bit of a clash to say the least. Mars finds it very difficult to function freely under the watchful eye of Saturn and what tends to happen is a repression or denial of the Martian characteristics. Anger may well be frowned upon; indeed all passionate outbursts are a no-no where Saturn is concerned, as the emotions should be controlled at all costs. Psychologically this aspect can pose problems because Mars wants to take action, but as soon as the starting point is neared Saturn kicks in and presents us with a load of 'what ifs?'. The result is a stop-start tendency or an inability to take control of one's own life and make things happen.

On a physical level this can translate itself as bone growths and swellings symbolising blocked energy, or inflammation and conditions such as arthritis symbolising a fear of moving forward and taking action. This aspect is one of paralysis – it is difficult to move with Saturn restricting the energy of Mars – so we may also see conditions of a paralytic nature (muscular paralysis or accidents that result in broken bones or paralysed areas of the body aren't uncommon). In order to prevent these conditions, it is essential that we don't become stuck. We must have courage in our convictions and take action despite our fears. With this aspect, any action is better than no action at all.

Repressed anger and sexual drives can cause problems and all emotions that are viewed as primitive or embarrassing need to be acknowledged and expressed constructively. Anything that enables the individual to become less rigid and restricted will be beneficial, so dancing and tai-chi are ideal. Martial arts are also a perfect way of disciplining and channelling the Mars energy.

It is important to remember that even the most challenging aspects offer a chance for growth, and this aspect when properly directed can be incredibly successful as the Martian energy becomes channelled constructively through planning, structure and perseverance.

HERBS AND SPICES: cayenne, comfrey, devil's claw, feverfew, ginger, horsetail, kombucha, nettle, wild oat

BACH FLOWERS: beech, centaury, elm, gentian, larch, olive, pine, rock water, vine, wild rose

COLOURS: orange, red

AROMATHERAPY OILS: basil, black pepper, neroli, patchouli, sandalwood, ylang ylang

VITAMINS AND MINERALS: calcium, cod liver oil, glucosamine with chondroitin, iron

IDEAL THERAPIES: dance, deep massage, martial arts, tai-chi

Mars–Uranus

KEYWORDS: Rebellious dynamite

The fiery energy of Mars combined with the electrical, unpredictable energy of Uranus creates fireworks. People with this aspect often have a short fuse and when lit it can lead to violent eruptions without much warning. People with this combination are often rebellious in nature, desire much freedom and must have life on their terms – sometimes at any cost. It could, then, be considered a selfish aspect, where the individual's desires overpower everyone else's.

On a physical level this erratic energy is most likely to result in accidents – through rushing, stress or lack of co-ordination. Far and away the biggest favour people with this aspect can do for themselves is to learn to relax and to remain calm in the face of provocation. Tension can manifest itself through muscular spasms, tears and twitches. The good side of this aspect is that anger is likely to be expressed rather than repressed, but if anger is frequent or directed at individuals then it won't make for a peaceful life. The channelling of energy through physical exercise is far better and a mind–body–spirit practice such as meditation or yoga will help to maintain balance and harmony.

HERBS AND SPICES: chamomile, motherwort, passion flower, skullcap, valerian

BACH FLOWERS: heather, holly, impatiens, rock rose, star of Bethlehem, vervain

COLOURS: blue, green, purple, turquoise

AROMATHERAPY OILS: chamomile, clary sage, frankincense, ginger, neroli, patchouli

VITAMINS AND MINERALS: magnesium, manganese

Mars–Neptune

KEYWORD: Egoless

An aspect between Mars and Neptune is not the best for good physical health, largely because the dissolving tendencies of Neptune can wreak havoc with the Martian immunity. It's rather like a tank trying to fire at its target through thick fog – it doesn't really know where the enemy is so it can't attack, or if it does it might end up injuring or destroying one of its own. All this can result in a weak or confused immune system, and so care needs to be taken to avoid things that tax our immunity and to look for ways of strengthening it through a healthy diet, plenty of sleep and relaxation. Drugs and alcohol can be especially detrimental with this aspect, as is overwork – people with this aspect need to pace themselves.

Physically, there can be a wasting of muscles and a susceptibility to infections. This is largely because psychologically there is a lack of identity – the barrier between you and me is thin or non-existent – and so the result is a drifting, or lack of direction and purpose in life. This sense of confusion about where one is heading can create a very lackadaisical approach or a reliance on drugs and alcohol, which only furthers the sense of apathy and confusion. This state of being is the flip side of what is essentially a search for spiritual unity and a shedding of the ego, because Mars–Neptune is rather a spiritual aspect, creating a desire for oneness and compassion. The unsuccessful attempts at achieving this are through drugs and alcohol: far better to achieve this aim by the use of spiritual practices such as yoga, meditation, tai-chi, music or art. These can link us into the higher dimensions so that we can temporarily forget ourselves, which is what this aspect is asking us to do.

HERBS AND SPICES: angelica root, basil, ginger, nettle, St John's wort, vervain, wild oat

BACH FLOWERS: centaury, clematis, gentian, larch, olive (especially for ME), wild oat, wild rose.

COLOURS: green, orange, red, turquoise

AROMATHERAPY OILS: basil, black pepper, cinnamon, frankincense, ginger, rosemary

VITAMINS AND MINERALS: co-enzyme Q10, iron, selenium, vitamin C, zinc

Mars–Pluto

KEYWORD: Power

The most powerful and potentially self-destructive aspect of all has to be Mars and Pluto. The intense power and destructive capabilities of Pluto are unleashed by the provocative warring stance of Mars and the results can be disastrous. Those with this aspect need to learn to control and channel their intensely powerful energy constructively before it destroys them. The good news is that if this energy can be focused positively it has enormous potential to bring powerful changes.

People with Mars–Pluto aspects must find a challenge – the bigger the better – something that they can become passionate about. Without passion, this aspect will create problems. This is largely because we are dealing with the two angry planets, and if the anger isn't directed at something external such as injustice or a project that can change lives, then the anger will become internalised or, alternatively, everyone and anything in the firing line will be obliterated.

On a physical level, this aspect relates to inflammations, infections and toxins. Abscesses and other ailments connected with poison, such as insect or animal bites, are symbolic of the angry, poisonous nature of the emotions and when the energy is not being used positively. Who or what are you feeling bitter about? Parasitical infections also reflect anger at the self.

HERBS AND SPICES: aloe vera, burdock, dong quai root, feverfew, slippery elm

BACH FLOWERS: beech, chicory, crab apple, heather, holly, impatiens, sweet chestnut, vine, willow

COLOURS: blue, orange, white

AROMATHERAPY OILS: chamomile, jasmine, juniper, lavender, patchouli, rose

VITAMINS AND MINERALS: iron, selenium, vitamin E, zinc

8

Jupiter –
The Meaning of Life

*'We shall not cease from exploration
And the end of all our exploring
Will be to arrive where we started
And know the place for the first time.'*
T.S. ELIOT

In traditional astrology, Jupiter has only a beneficial personality. Big, bright, bold and bountiful, he tends to make life easy for us. We all look forward to our Jupiter transits for they are renowned for bringing us gifts and good fortune. Likewise, in our natal charts we tend to be luckier and more confident wherever Jupiter resides, in all his resplendent glory. It would be hard to imagine, then, that a planet such as Jupiter with all its associated good fortune and benevolence could have an adverse aspect on health. But it's important to remember that the philosophy of astrology and health is that the creation of well-being depends on the successful expression of energy as a whole, and that any planet, whether traditionally deemed good or not, can cause problems if repressed. Jupiter is no exception. He needs to be able to expand – rules and restrictions have a detrimental effect on his broadminded, adventurous personality. However, first and foremost, Jupiter needs meaning.

Jupiter and the quest for the Holy Grail

Jupiter does have a serious side and in our charts he reveals what gives us meaning. For this reason Jupiter is spiritual in essence. Jupiter in Libra, the 7th house or aspecting Venus, for example, would mean that life without love would be meaningless. For someone who has Jupiter in Taurus or in the 2nd house, money would assume more importance than for the average person. In Cancer, the 4th house or nestling with the Moon, it would be the family and children that would rank most highly. It is important to be aware of what Jupiter is doing in our charts so that we can accept whatever area of life we need to give us meaning and not feel guilty about it.

Jupiter's influence is protective and supportive, but it can also be enlarging or excessive. In other words, a stressfully aspected or prominent Jupiter can be too much of a good thing.

Physiological correspondences

Jupiter's main function is the liver. This is because the protective influence of this planet is synonymous with the detoxifying role of the liver, which protects the rest of the body from the harmful effects of toxins and chemicals. Jupiter also governs fat metabolism and the production of bile and urea – the task of the gall bladder. Since Jupiter is predominantly about growth, he is also connected with the growth hormone.

The liver

In Chinese medicine, the liver is the storehouse of anger. How on earth then do we equate anger with the wonderfully happy and uplifting qualities traditionally associated with Jupiter? Perhaps the answer lies in understanding that repressed anger can become depression, and depression often arises from a lack of purpose and meaning. And this is where the toxic overload that our livers have to deal with comes in. If our life lacks meaning or purpose, if we don't know why we're here, if there doesn't seem much point to life, then we're far more likely to intoxicate ourselves with various addictions, such as alcoholism, excessive sugar and fat intake, smoking and drug misuse. Even television is a suitable way of numbing inner pain. Linking anger and depression with a lack of purpose thus makes perfect sense. We may be angry at ourselves for not living out our true purpose. It works the other way round too: whenever the liver is sluggish (due to high levels of toxins), depression is the result. The liver gives us life (take away the 'r' and we're left with 'live').

So if our life leaves a lot to be desired, our liver may suffer, because without meaning we don't really care whether we live or die and so we will commit slow suicide with various addictions or forms of excess, all in an attempt to give us the high that is naturally lacking.

Jupiter is the planet of excess and greed, and frequently when this planet is over-pronounced or adversely aspected we fail to recognise our boundaries. We may push ourselves beyond our limits or indulge in excessive behaviour or habits. If we don't know when to stop, our liver will take the brunt and, since the liver repairs damage while we sleep, depriving ourselves of a healthy 7 or 8 hours adds a further strain. Also, if we are damaging our liver, we may wake up very tired since it won't be able to do its job properly while we sleep.

Gall bladder

The function of the gall bladder is to collect the bile from the liver, which then helps facilitate the digestive process. Bile is a bitter green substance so it's hardly surprising that we've come to associate the word gall with anger or audacity – 'she had the gall to say *I* was stupid!'. Since gallstones occur more frequently in women than men, and again more often in married women with families, we can see how gallstones might reflect a repressed audacity or boldness. We have to curtail ourselves, be a responsible parent and spouse, and set ourselves firm limits. As such, the lack of freedom to be ourselves and do what we'd really like to do can lead to repressed anger, which can then lead to the formation of gallstones. In these cases, we need to acknowledge where we're being curtailed, and try to find some way to compromise so that we can still be true to ourselves without dispensing with our responsibilities. (See Jupiter–Saturn on page 87 for more on this.)

Living in harmony with Jupiter – finding purpose and meaning

In order to live in harmony with our Jupiter, we need to ensure that we are treading the middle path. It's all too easy with Jupiter to fall into a pattern of excess and self-indulgence. William Blake wrote 'the road of excess leads to the palace of wisdom'. However, with such a philosophy there is a price to be paid and perhaps a better philosophy might be 'the road of experience leads to the palace of wisdom'. Jupiter is always prone to excess – a negatively aspected Jupiter is never satisfied. Things are never good enough and we are always left wanting more. Our appetites are voracious and rarely sated, but what Jupiter is really asking of us is to fill the inner void so that we are full within, and no longer searching for fulfilment on the outside.

Meaning

In order to fill our inner void, we first need to feel our lives have a purpose. If we don't, we feel terribly empty and that's when compensation through excess becomes tempting. We can find meaning by connecting to God or the universal energy that connects and sustains all living things. When we connect to this force we realise that all life has meaning. At the same time, when we consider the vastness of the universe, we humbly realise that we are like a grain of sand on a 10-mile beach – though each grain is precious and equal to all the others.

Each of us suffers low points in life, or even times when life seems to lack any point at all. This is when we need to look for the opportunity contained within the redundancy or breakdown of a relationship. Opportunity is one of Jupiter's keywords and, by adopting the perspective of when one door closes another one opens, we keep our gaze fixed on the possibilities of tomorrow rather than on the regrets of yesterday.

Growth and adventure

Jupiter pushes us towards growth – if we're not growing mentally and spiritually by expanding our minds and pushing ourselves to experience life to the full, we will encourage negative growth in the form of weight gain. Most of us live within our comfort zones – especially as we get older. When young, we take more risks, are prepared to do without our creature comforts and generally push our own boundaries. As we settle into certain patterns such as marriage and long-term jobs with mortgages and families, it becomes increasingly hard to maintain that early sense of adventure. Instead of venturing out to try something new, we pacify ourselves with television and pre-packaged foods. We follow the path of least resistance where everything is done for us or made as easy and unadventurous as possible.

This isn't music to Jupiter's ears, who desperately needs to be experiencing life and, if need be, taking the odd risk. Remember how exhilarated you felt when you had successfully done something that was initially very scary, whether it was your first presentation to a group, uprooting to a different part of the country or world, or taking a gamble and leaving a job you hated for one you loved? Even going to a fairground and riding the roller-coaster can reconnect us with our adventurous, fun-loving spirit. Taking up a new hobby or joining a club can initially be a little daunting, but these are the challenges that create inner growth and give our lives greater meaning.

Gratitude

The act of being grateful is a spiritual one that is often overlooked. We tend to take so much for granted (a typical Jupiter response), for example our health, our families, loved ones, home, finances, a kind word from a stranger, food in the cupboards, loving pets, our freedom – the list is endless. When we are experiencing the negative side of Jupiter we don't notice what we've already got because our eyes are firmly fixed on the horizon, looking for what we might be missing. A classic Jupiter (and Sagittarian) perception is of the grass being greener on the other side. If we are forever looking over the fence to see what our neighbours have, we're not noticing the beauty of what we already possess. If not kept in check, this can lead to resentment and a feeling of forever chasing our tails as we keep searching and lusting after more and more. When we notice and appreciate all that we have, the ensuing wave of inner fulfilment is so great that we don't want anything more.

Your Jupiter is out of balance when:

- O You feel that life has no meaning
- O You tend to overdo it – whether 'it' is drugs, burning the candle at both ends, overeating or gambling
- O To you, big is beautiful and so you must have the biggest and best of everything
- O You find it difficult to think of things to be thankful for
- O You think you know it all and could be perceived as arrogant
- O You have no spiritual beliefs or philosophies, which leaves you feeling empty

To increase the strength of your Jupiter and your liver:

○ Embrace the unknown – see life as a big adventure, much as a child does

○ Identify and live out your purpose – you are a unique person and have a unique reason for being here

○ Know that just as every flower, tree and bird has a right to exist, so do you

○ Identify the things that give your life meaning and focus more energy on them

○ Know your limits, don't push your body to excess

○ Be generous to yourself and others

○ Expand your mind through travel, philosophy or study

○ Develop the philosophy 'less is more'

○ Appreciate what you have – keep a gratitude journal. By focusing more on the good things you have, you'll not only feel better inside but you'll also attract more of the universe's bounty.

○ Take the occasional risk – do something daring, exciting or uncertain

Aspects to Jupiter (including transits)

Jupiter–Sun
See page 33.

Jupiter–Moon
See page 44.

Jupiter–Mercury
See page 56.

Jupiter–Venus
See page 66.

Jupiter–Mars

See page 77.

Jupiter–Saturn

KEYWORD: Restriction

Jupiter is expansive, Saturn is restrictive, so it's fair to say these two don't get on at all well. If care isn't taken, Saturn can have an adverse effect on the liver and gall bladder, resulting in gallstones. The metabolism may also be slowed down, resulting in battles with weight. All this reflects a psychological rigidity or restriction, where freedom and adventure are sacrificed for a safe and predictable life. There may also be a tendency towards long-term or chronic diseases, because Jupiter's protective function is being impaired by Saturn. Again this is reflective of a restrictive, rigid or overly safe frame of mind. To alleviate the tension of this aspect, we need to adopt a certain amount of freedom, adventure and risk, while at the same time setting sensible limits and precautions.

HERBS AND SPICES: barberry, dandelion root, parsley root, peppermint leaves

BACH FLOWER: rock water

COLOURS: orange, yellow

AROMATHERAPY OILS: cedarwood, cumin, geranium, juniper, peppermint, sandalwood

VITAMINS AND MINERALS: cholin, lecithin

Jupiter–Uranus

KEYWORD: Excitability

Impulsive excess lies at the root of any problem induced by these two planets. Uranus's love of the unusual and need for excitement fuels Jupiter's lust for adventure, thrills and spills and greed, so that the appetites are rather voracious or can swing from one extreme to another. A tendency to overdo things can cause health problems so care should be taken to act in moderation, otherwise the liver may suffer with colic or the gastrointestinal tract can have spasmodic pains and problems.

HERBS AND SPICES: dandelion root, peppermint leaves, valerian, yellow dock root

BACH FLOWERS: vervain, wild oat

COLOURS: blue, purple, yellow

AROMATHERAPY OILS: benzoin, clary sage, ginger, neroli

VITAMINS AND MINERALS: biotin, cholin, chromium, magnesium, manganese

Jupiter–Neptune

KEYWORD: Aimlessness

Here the metabolism may be weak, resulting in food particles not being broken down correctly, which in turn leads to gas and abdominal distension. Tissues may become waterlogged, giving a feeling or a look of heaviness. Overeating is also common with this aspect, which may be acting to numb the inner emptiness that is usually revealed as a lack of purpose. When we are clear about what we want and where we're going, these physical problems should dissipate.

HERBS AND SPICES: burdock, fennel, parsley root, peppermint

BACH FLOWER: wild oat

COLOURS: red, yellow

AROMATHERAPY OILS: cypress, eucalyptus, geranium, juniper, lavender, pine, rosemary

VITAMINS AND MINERALS: potassium, sodium

Jupiter–Pluto

KEYWORD: Greed

This aspect can be positive in health terms, denoting strong recuperative and protective powers. However, the urge to achieve something big or to be a big powerful person can lead to compulsive eating, overeating, or eating disorders. Obviously, then, with this aspect weight can be a problem, as can gout from too much rich food. The compulsive nature of Pluto can feed the self-indulgence aspect of Jupiter so we consume anything that's going – food, alcohol, drugs – and the more the merrier. What we need to recognise with this aspect is that we are already big and powerful – we don't need a huge bank account, car or house or a mega-successful business to validate our worth. When we can recognise this, any desire to consume more than is healthy, both literally and figuratively, will diminish.

HERBS AND SPICES: burdock, dandelion root, fennel, nettle, yellow dock root

BACH FLOWERS: vervain, vine, water violet

COLOURS: pale blue, pale green, white

AROMATHERAPY OILS: cypress, fennel, geranium, lavender, patchouli, rosemary, sage, thyme

VITAMINS AND MINERALS: vitamin E

9

Saturn – Getting Real

'Sow an act, and you reap a habit. Sow a habit,
and you reap a character. Sow a character,
and you reap a destiny.'
[CHARLES READ]

Mention Saturn to any student of astrology, and the response will be almost invariably the same – grimaces, frowns and a peculiar enthusiasm to move on to another topic of conversation as quickly as possible. Likewise anyone who knows anything about astrology who is about to experience a Saturn transit will spend the preceding six months in a state of apprehensive anxiety. We can't wait for our Jupiter returns, but Saturn – no thanks. Why does this poor beleaguered planet – traditionally referred to as the great malefic – have such a bad reputation, especially relating to our health, and is it justified? And if it's as bad as it's made out, shouldn't we try forming a better relationship with him in order to give ourselves an easier time?

The Karmic Lord

Perhaps we should start with a look at Saturn's functions in our lives in order to answer the above questions. Saturn's main function is to bring form and structure to our lives; without it we fall apart – physically and mentally. Saturn brings order where there's chaos and rules where there's rebellion. For this reason he is known as the Lord of Karma and governs universal law. In other words Saturn ensures that whatever we give out, we get back. Since none of us is perfect, it's hardly surprising that we attract negative events from time to time. And this is why most of us run a million miles when we see him coming. Unless we're paragons of virtue, Saturn can be an uncomfortable reminder that we still have a lot of learning to do.

Saturn is associated with time, so his results do not appear overnight as they may do with the Sun, Venus, Mars or Jupiter. The wait is often well worth it, though, as what is achieved or learned is permanent. Everything about this planet is slow, careful, measured, ordered, structured and, yes, sometimes a little dull. Taken to extremes, the planet can result in rigidity, a lack of freedom and spontaneity and restriction. Saturn doesn't sit very well with our society, which is largely youth-orientated, fast-paced and disposable. We don't value age and maturity, and we certainly don't have much time for patience – especially when it comes to illness. We'd much rather drown out the messages our symptoms are trying to impart with suppressive drugs. Therefore, our own individual Saturns are not being given the respect they need or deserve. This can cause problems for us, not least in health terms, as prolonged or chronic poor health often has its roots in a Saturnian issue that we have thus far failed to deal with. Since Saturn is psychological in nature, playing a huge part in forming our patterns and beliefs about ourselves and the world, we need to be aware of the mental baggage we carry around that could be hindering us from having a happier life.

Physiological correspondences

Because Saturn is largely concerned with structure, it is the structures of our bodies that are ruled by him. These are the skin, teeth, bones, skeletal system, spine and joints. Afflictions to Saturn in the chart can result in bone problems such as osteoporosis, fractures and breaks. Chronic skin problems, back pain and arthritis are the other main Saturn ailments. All long-term chronic diseases and symptoms are Saturnian in nature, as are blockages and obstructions.

On a psychological level, the heavy, oppressive nature of Saturn can lead to depression.

Arthritis

The muscles, bones and joints give us the ability to move. Problems in these areas make it difficult to move with ease. Arthritis is a hugely common disease in which the joints become inflamed, making movement difficult and sometimes unbearable. Also linked to arthritis is stiffness in the joints. It is easy to see how this stiffness is reflected in the unbending, rigid attitude of Saturn. Pain or stiffness in the joints is symbolic of a stiff attitude or an inability to bend, and in these cases we may need to ask ourselves where we're being rigid, restrictive or critical.

It is noticeable that arthritis is more common in elderly people, as by then our habits are more fixed and our attitudes, beliefs and thought patterns have become set like cement. This is why it's vitally important to maintain a flexible outlook on life. We are often amazed when we see people in their 70s engaged in active sports, but this is precisely what we should be doing if we want to remain youthful.

The skin

Our skin reflects what's going on inside and is the greatest barometer of our health. If we aren't getting enough sleep or taking in enough fluid or eating healthily, our skin reflects this through lacklustre greyness or a drawn, hollow look. Our skin is also our boundary – it defines where we end and the outside world begins. It protects us from infections and represents our identity. Many skin conditions do indeed reinforce our boundaries and sense of isolation: rashes, burns, acne, eczema and cold sores all keep people at bay, either because it's uncomfortable or painful for us to be touched or because we feel self-conscious so we hide. If this is the case, we may need to look at fear of sharing ourselves with others – a classic Saturn problem.

Depression

Because depression is not very well understood by the medical establishment, sufferers tend to receive little help and support. Depression is difficult to understand because it is not physical in origin, even though it is often accompanied by 'heavy' symptoms such as muscular heaviness and aches, migraines and headaches, and tiredness and lethargy. Since Saturn is the heavy, serious planet, it is often closely associated with depression, and sufferers will usually have Saturn pronounced in their charts or be undergoing a Saturn transit – especially to the Sun or Moon.

We need to remember, though, that this is the negative manifestation of Saturnian energy – it has become blocked, frustrated or twisted. In order to use Saturn energy correctly we need to have something to work towards – a goal, a purpose, some sort of direction. Saturn rules Capricorn, and Capricorn is the sign of ambition and success. Capricorns are never happier than when they are constructively employed and when they have something to achieve. It is very difficult for a Capricorn or Saturn person to sit doing nothing or to engage in purely frivolous pursuits. Such people thrive on hard work, challenge, responsibility and achieving. A depressed person, by contrast, feels there is nothing much worth living for, no purpose, no meaning, no goals and nothing to achieve. By discovering what motivates us and actively pursuing it, we can overcome depression and its associated feelings of worthlessness, guilt and emptiness.

Living in harmony with Saturn – responsibility and goal setting

Saturn is not always the easiest planet to live in harmony with – it requires us to be responsible, but not overly so, hardworking, but not so much that we forget about the important things in life. But most of all, Saturn requires us to face up to our fears and insecurities, which is quite possibly the hardest thing we ever have to do. If we surrender to our fears and let them govern our lives, being afraid to take risks or try for things that run the risk of failure, we can get depressed.

Responsibility and karma

It's not always easy taking responsibility for our lives – especially if they're not working too well. However, Saturn always holds us accountable and if we shirk our responsibilities for too long or act in an irresponsible fashion, we will usually reap what we've sown at a later date – usually around an important Saturn transit when all our chickens come home to roost. This is when we're most likely to get caught out or when our past catches up with us. Saturn always likes to remind us of our debts and karmic obligations, which is why his presence often feels so heavy and obstructive. We're not allowed to pass through the gateway until we've learned our lesson, which can be as easy or as difficult as we choose to make it.

So in order to keep Saturn happy, we must be responsible for our actions and, whenever we do act, bear in mind the consequences. If we're 'not prepared to do the time, we shouldn't commit the crime' is Saturn's stern but fair message. Therefore, if you're about to embark on an affair, fiddle your tax return or con the insurance company, be prepared for the consequences. We may think we can get away with certain things but, as the song goes, 'the eyes of truth are always watching you'.

Achievement and perfectionism

Have you ever noticed – within either yourself or others – that when a goal is achieved the initial elation is followed by a mood slump? Achievement is a funny thing – we think we want something more than anything else and then when we get it we feel 'so what?'. Post-achievement blues comes because we have climbed a mountain and then feel confused and frustrated because we don't know what to do next. This is especially likely to be the case if we are achievement orientated because we're often unconsciously trying to impress a parent figure. We go all out for success, get it and still feel as empty inside as we did before. Therefore it's crucial to ascertain who the achievement is for. Ideally, we want to achieve something because it resonates with who we are and it feels like the right thing to do. There is a big difference between the therapist whose goal is to set up a healing centre for the benefit of others, and the eternal student who adds another string of letters after his or her name every few years.

The opposite side of the coin is the person who is too afraid of failure or not achieving perfection to even try. If this is you, try asking what is beneath the fear of failure and how you would feel if you did fail. And, just as importantly, what would be the repercussions of your success? Replace these fears by understanding that each 'failure' is a lesson or experience that takes you closer to your eventual success. We have to know what doesn't work before we can realise what does.

Planning and goal setting

Once we have something in mind that we'd like to achieve, we need to take measured steps towards getting there. People who write down their goals and then decide upon a series of steps to achieving them are at least 90 per cent more likely to be successful than those who have a vague notion floating around inside their heads. Saturn loves structure, so create a plan for your ambition. Saturn also loves patience and persistence, so don't give up at the first hurdle and be prepared for delays, which are the universe's way of making sure you're really ready.

Breaking free of limits

It is very easy for us to over-identify with Saturn in some ways because he represents our comfort zone, and most of us are very partial to sticking with what is safe and known. As we get older, our beliefs and opinions become more and more entrenched, which is why dancing, yoga and tai-chi are absolutely invaluable for anyone suffering from a Saturn complaint or anyone with Saturn or Capricorn strong in their charts. We need to avoid becoming rigid and narrow-minded. We need to practise the childlike habit of greeting life with an open and enthusiastic mind. With Saturn it is all too easy to become cynical and hard-edged. We look for the dark instead of the light and see what's wrong with the world instead of what's right. We limit ourselves and say 'that's not possible – I could never do that'. Saturn does not think big, and if Saturn is strong in our charts we need to remind ourselves that our negative perceptions of life and what's achievable are not necessarily absolute truths.

Since the area of our charts where Saturn resides will reveal our fears and insecurities, we can become more aware of where, how and why we hold ourselves back. Saturn in Libra, the 7th house or aspecting Venus will highlight fears and insecurities to do with relationships. Perhaps we don't feel very loveable so we unconsciously attract partners who don't treat us too well, or we may be so fearful on our own that we rush into marriage or become overly dependent on our partner.

Wherever Saturn lies in our charts it is a reminder to take on a more responsible attitude and to face up to our fears and insecurities in that realm of life.

Your Saturn is out of balance when:

○ You're afraid to take a risk in case it doesn't work out

○ You try and control everything that goes on around you, from other people to situations and your environment

○ You feel uncomfortable when people act in a wild or unpredictable fashion

○ You don't like your plans being changed at the last minute

○ Your reaction to playing games is one of disdain

○ You don't do creative or playful things because you're 'not that sort of person'

○ Your life is very safe and comfortable, but also rather dull and boring

○ You don't think you're clever enough, good enough or sexy enough or whatever other limiting belief keeps you down

○ You always have to be doing something useful or productive – you find it very difficult to just sit and do 'nothing'

○ You suffer from depression – usually a sign that something needs to change – perhaps a situation that you're in or your attitude to it

To increase the strength of your Saturn and the health of your bones and joints:

○ Confront your fears and insecurities head on – don't let them rule your life or prevent you from living life to the full

○ Take up a fluid pursuit such as yoga, dance or tai-chi to keep you mentally and physically supple

○ Keep challenging your own thoughts, opinions and beliefs; by being open to change we maintain a youthful spirit

○ If you suffer from depression, try taking St John's wort. If the depression is severe, consider seeing a therapist or counsellor to help you get to the root cause.

○ Break out of your comfort zone and keep pushing your own boundaries: try doing something a little challenging from time to time

○ Identify those areas of your life in which you're rigid and fearful. Where do you limit yourself and consider yourself unworthy?

○ Don't be afraid of failure for it is merely another stepping stone across the river to success. Read Susan Jeffers' *Feel the Fear and Do It Anyway*.

○ Learn to praise instead of condemning and criticising yourself

○ Nip negative thoughts in the bud and replace them with positive affirmations

○ Wear the colour orange to offset the heavy, slow and dour vibration of Saturn

Aspects to Saturn (including transits)

Saturn–Sun

See page 33.

Saturn–Moon

See page 45.

Saturn–Mercury

See page 56.

Saturn–Venus

See page 67.

Saturn–Mars

See page 77.

Saturn–Jupiter

See page 87.

Saturn–Uranus

KEYWORD: Chaos

Here we have planetary opposites – Saturn who likes to play it safe, by the book and with reverence for authority meets the unpredictable Uranus who has nothing but contempt for authority, rules and regulations. The result is often internal stress as the personality rigorously clings to one side or the other.

This aspect is said to attract catastrophes of one form or another – the car accident, the bankruptcy, or the sudden collapse of the marriage. When Saturn and Uranus get together it often looks as though life deals a succession of cruel blows – that fate is against us. What's really going on though is the outer manifestation of internal conflicts. If we stay within the soul-destroying job out of safety and security, we attract a redundancy. If we remain in an unhappy marriage, our partner runs off with a lover. It's very easy to fall into victim mode here, because it appears that life is being cruel to us, but really it is only reflecting what we feel inside. When we realise this, we will become free of the negative elements of this aspect because we'll have realised our own power. Until we can do this we are liable to attract all kinds of chaos, from accidents – particularly broken bones, fractures and breaks, injuries to the spine, and eruptions with the skin and teeth – to little disasters and situations that periodically pull the rug from under our feet.

HERBS AND SPICES: angelica root, burdock, chamomile, valerian

BACH FLOWERS: rock rose, star of Bethlehem, walnut, wild oat

COLOURS: indigo, purple, white

AROMATHERAPY OILS: cedarwood, chamomile, geranium, lavender, patchouli, sandalwood

Saturn–Neptune

KEYWORD: Dissolution

The planet of structure meets the planet of disintegration, and the result is not always pleasant. Saturn represents boundaries and limits: Neptune wants to merge and become one. Saturn needs to know exactly where he stands: Neptune doesn't really care. Obviously, this aspect can cause problems on both a psychological and a physical level. There may be a split within the personality whereby the Saturn part of the self tries to maintain control while the Neptune part seeks to undermine that control. The result can be a reliance on alcohol that provides a loss of control or an escape from the tight constraints of having to be in control. Depression may be a feature as Neptune undermines all that Saturn has worked for, and can result in a lack of purpose, uncertainty or a sense of falling apart. Anxiety, complexes, neuroses and phobias are possible with this aspect, largely because Neptune undermines the sense of self and ability to achieve in the world.

Physically, the structure of the body – the bones, skin and teeth – may be weak and prone to problems. Osteoporosis and osteomalacia are examples of bone problems.

To counteract this aspect, there needs to be a balance between hard work and planning to achieve one's dreams and visions, and understanding that status and material success do not define us or bring permanent happiness.

HERBS AND SPICES: comfrey, horsetail, St John's wort, vervain, wild oat

BACH FLOWERS: agrimony, clematis, larch, mimulus, wild oat, wild rose

COLOURS: dark blue, pink, purple, red (for motivation), yellow

AROMATHERAPY OILS: basil, bergamot, eucalyptus, melissa, orange, pine, rose

VITAMINS AND MINERALS: calcium, magnesium, phosphorus, sulphur, vitamin D

Saturn–Pluto

KEYWORD: Loss

Here we have two giants battling it out for supremacy and the result can be ugly. Both planets are concerned with control and power but whereas Saturn seeks to maintain what is safe and known, Pluto seeks to destroy it. Therefore people born with this aspect can have rather traumatic lives where every so often the rug is whipped out from under their feet leaving them to deal with sudden and often shocking losses. The positive side of this aspect is one of wisdom and an understanding that nothing stays the same, thus creating inner security. Because of the high level of fear associated with this aspect, weight gain as a psychological protective mechanism may be a problem. There may also be a hardening or calcification of bones. Constipation may feature as there is a natural tendency to 'hold on' through a fear of loss. With this aspect, the most important attitude we can develop is one of letting go. Trust and acceptance, enabling us to embrace life instead of resisting it, come a close second.

HERBS AND SPICES: vervain, yellow dock root

BACH FLOWERS: chestnut bud, chicory, crab apple, gentian, gorse, mimulus, mustard, star of Bethlehem, sweet chestnut

COLOURS: lilac, turquoise, white

AROMATHERAPY OILS: cypress, geranium, jasmine, juniper, melissa, rose

VITAMINS AND MINERALS: silica, vitamin D

PHILOSOPHY: trust and let go

10

Uranus –
The Spark of Life

'Life is either a wonderful adventure or nothing.'
HELEN KELLER

After the safety and security of Saturn comes the mad, crazy genius of Uranus. He has no time for rules and regulations and will set about causing anarchy as soon as possible. If Saturn is the right-wing politician or the police officer, Uranus is the rock 'n' roll rebel or the animal rights activist. They observe each other with a certain amount of disdain and a total lack of understanding. Uranus seeks to challenge the status quo, because he's well aware that as we get older we can all too easily become entrenched in our beliefs and overly set in our ways, with the result that we slowly begin to close down to life. It's Uranus's job to ensure that we remember what life is supposed to be about – a glorious, exciting adventure – and every so often he will remind us of this in no uncertain terms. This is why around the age of 40, when Uranus comes around to oppose the natal position, people tend to break free of their previous limitations. We may suddenly fall in love with all the passion of a teenager, or we may abruptly decide that we're not going to put up with the rotten nine-to-five job any more and find a new lease of life as a painter. For the Saturnian person who depends on life being safe and ordered, the ensuing chaos of a visit from Uranus can be a nightmare, but only because we've resisted what needs to change for too long.

Uranus and the quest for truth

There is a saying in astrology: 'If you don't do your chart, your chart will do you.' This is never more so than with Uranus as it's his responsibility to ensure that we remain true to ourselves at the highest level, and yet it often appears that the events which occur out of the blue have nothing to do with us. But Uranus is distinctly metaphysical and he merely mirrors what we are repressing. In other words, if we hate our job but stick with it through fear or laziness, Uranus will orchestrate the redundancy or the sacking. It may seem unfair at first glance but at a deeper level the freedom and opportunity for change is what we really wanted. Likewise with the unhappy marriage: if we decide to endure it for our children or for the material benefits or through fear of being alone, we can't bemoan our fate if our spouse has an affair or runs off with someone else.

The purpose of Uranus, then, is to encourage us to be true to ourselves. Uranus has no time for dishonesty and only if we're living a lie do we need to worry about the physical implications of Uranus.

Physiological correspondences

Uranus chiefly governs the nervous system and ensures the smooth running of all the rhythmic processes, from our beating heart to our digestive process. When we are out of sync with Uranus we are likely to suffer from palpitations, tremors, spasms, numbness, neuralgia, tics and twitches. At a more serious level we may have a mental breakdown, a seizure or a stroke.

The nervous system

Uranus is the electrical spark that kick-starts life into action and without that spark there would be no life. Similarly, the nervous system functions via electrical impulses, and if there is a fault the whole system can temporarily shut down.

The nervous system is the hub from where all the body's movements are controlled and co-ordinated. Think of it as the control centre at an airport: the people inside are monitoring and sending information to their planes in the sky, hopefully keeping everything running smoothly. Two separate parts are functioning as one unit. The nervous system receives information from the senses and sends it to the brain – the big boss of the nervous system – where it is then processed. This information is then translated into thoughts, actions and, ultimately, beliefs and emotions. The information is sent back via the spinal cord and then out to all other parts of the body along the nerve pathways, rather like routes on a map leading off from a big city centre.

The pineal gland, which governs sexual and mental function, is very interesting from the point of view of Uranian function because the it is the link between physical and non-physical, between spirit and matter (Descartes described it as the seat of the soul). Uranus is also in charge of linking spirit with matter, as in the case of channelling information from universal sources or other beings on to paper. Automatic writing, intuition, clairvoyance and messages from beyond the grave are all communication of a Uranian nature – they come from sources higher than the self. The genius who suddenly knows the complex mathematical answer to a problem, or the more down-to-earth person who nevertheless occasionally has flashes of inspiration, is in Uranian mode.

The nervous system then links the mind with the body, and problems here show that we have lost some sort of connection between ourselves and the world around us. For example, a simple headache could be caused by overloading our nervous system, leading to stress and tension, or it could be the consequence of trying to control others or situations that can't or shouldn't be controlled. The metaphorical result of banging our head against a brick wall is likely to be a headache. Either way we are out of touch with our inner needs and not going with the flow.

Circulatory disorders

Any problem with our circulation implies that we are becoming blocked, that we are resisting whatever needs to change. If you have circulatory problems ascertain whether you're going with the flow or not, or whether you're the sort of person that needs to control situations and people, or whether you're resisting some change that needs to be made. A blood clot is reflective of becoming stuck and resistant to change. Strokes also relate to the circulatory system (as well as the nervous system) and many older people get strokes because they have by this time become more fixed and fearful of change. They may fear what's left of their future – being put in a home can arouse as much fear as can anything else that disrupts their previously safe life.

The above is largely true of any condition that results in paralysis, whether it be long-term paralysis after a stroke or accident or whether it's more temporary due to an injury or a bout of illness that lays us up for a week or more.

High blood pressure is also a form of resistance because we aren't going with the flow when we're angry or stressed. The constant state of inner tension that leads to high blood pressure reflects a going against the grain and the effects of trying to swim against the current are psychological and emotional angst. High blood pressure is a leading cause of heart attacks and strokes, so if you suffer from it resolve to incorporate more serenity and balance into your life.

Low blood pressure is a reluctance or fear to plunge into life. The holding-back nature of such a person is reflected in the weakness of their blood, which represents joy. Feeling dizzy, weak or overwhelmed suggests a difficulty in coping with life's pressures, demands and challenges. We need to toughen up a little so that we have not just the inner strength but also the enthusiasm to cope with life in all its colours.

Accidents

At first glance it may seem strange to include accidents as they are things that happen to us rather than the result of our minds affecting our bodies. Or are they? This question takes us back to the beginning of the chapter when we considered Uranus as the malefic force that reveals our inner discontent. Accidents are typically Uranian: they happen suddenly and can turn our world upside-down if severe enough.

When we are discontented, seriously stressed or on the wrong path, we will often attract an event that is severe enough to force us to stop for a while, turn inwards and contemplate what we're doing and why.

The key question to ask yourself if involved in any type of accident is in which area of life you are not being true to yourself. Are you in the wrong job, or the wrong relationship? Are you denying an aspect of yourself? Do you know your purpose in life and are you fulfilling it? If not, what steps can you take to discover it and make it a reality? If you are very stressed, what has caused you to be so out of flow with yourself and the universe, and is the cause of the stress really worth it?

Although difficult to accept and deal with at first, accidents can serve the very useful purpose of reconnecting us with what we came here to do and, perhaps just as importantly, of realigning ourselves with the person we are deep down inside.

The best remedies for all these Uranian symptoms are those that ground and calm us, from walking, massage and gentle cycling to yoga and meditation. Magnesium and manganese are the minerals that can help Uranian conditions since they help muscular function, keeping cramps and spasms at bay.

Living in harmony with Uranus – freedom, originality, self-honesty

Uranus is one of the more difficult planets to harmonise with, largely because the nature of today's society is anti-Uranian – safe, structured and ordered. Anyone seen to be acting differently is frowned upon or even ostracised, so it takes courage to rebel or to tread a different path. However, we don't need to dance down the street naked to keep Uranus happy, we just have to take action whenever we feel bored, frustrated or trapped.

Being true to yourself

It may be a phrase much bandied about these days, but being true to ourselves is much trickier than we might first imagine. Why? Because it may involve upsetting or disappointing others. For the son whose parents are expecting a top-class barrister, it may be too frightening a concept for him to pull out of law school to follow his dream of being an artist. Or the dismally unhappy wife who stays within a hollow marriage because she fears that if she doesn't her husband might fall apart, or her family might condemn her. Our fear of other people's reactions is often the reason why we stay put, but to do so will only lead to greater frustration and more unhappiness. We need to ask ourselves the question, whose life is it anyway?

And if it's not fear of what other people might think, perhaps we don't believe enough in ourselves to make the change. The stressful job might be taking its toll on our health, but if we don't feel we're good enough for anything else, we may stay stuck and waiting for disaster to strike in the form of physical collapse or redundancy.

It's always fear that gets in the way of making change – fear of others, fear of not having enough money, fear of what we might lose (or gain). But the alternative is a kind of self-imposed prison, with each day being the same as the last and a growing sense of frustration as our daily companion. So we do need to be honest about whatever might not be working in our lives and either make an effort to fix it or have the courage to change it. Remember that Uranus can't tolerate that which has become stale, stifling and mundane. Uranus needs to feel that we are experiencing life not just existing. So if you want to prevent the Uranian lightning bolt from striking, do what you need to do to make life a little more exhilarating.

Making a difference

So you thought Uranus was a selfish planet – inconsiderate of others and deliberately going his own way? Well, as is always the case with this planet, it's a bit of a yes and a bit of a no. The unpredictable nature of this planet means he can swing both ways and in all directions. Yes, he's inconsiderate in the sense that he will go his own way regardless, feeling that those with a problem with that should deal with it. But he's far from inconsiderate when it comes to the rights of all living beings, which is one of his main concerns. Perhaps we need to redefine our concept of selfish because, at the end of the day, Uranus is only concerned with honesty, and is it selfish to be honest?

Honesty also involves exposing those who take away or diminish the rights of others. Greenpeace, Amnesty International, Friends of the Earth and Compassion in World Farming are all Uranian organisations concerned with the rights of people, animals and the planet and exposing those who seek to exploit, lie and cheat. But you don't have to be part of a charitable organisation to fulfil your Uranian need to improve society. Perhaps your job enables you to make a difference to people's lives – social work, caring for the disadvantaged, alternative healing or anything radical or unusual that puts others at the forefront. Maybe you have some sort of vision that will help improve society. Or maybe it's enough for you to make a regular donation to Uranian causes – not everyone is Uranian enough to be out there on the front line, but if you can do at least something, you'll probably be a whole lot happier for it.

Your Uranus is out of balance when:

○ You feel mentally overloaded or scattered

○ You can't sit still

○ You go out of your way to be different

○ Others are put off by your unpredictable or shocking behaviour

○ You are a law unto yourself and as such may be unreliable

○ You deliberately flout rules and regulations because you don't like authority

○ You feel restless but don't know why

○ You enjoy provoking or winding people up

To increase the strength of your Uranus and your nervous system:

○ Take regular time out to relax – don't wait till overload stage before doing something about it

○ Try to welcome change instead of fearing or resisting it

○ Dare to be different: you are unique – demonstrate it

○ Don't let yourself become stifled: whether it's a weekend away or your own private space, create pockets of freedom whenever possible

○ Treat mini-accidents as warnings – a bigger one might be round the corner if you don't slow down or make changes

○ Limit your time and use of electrical items – especially mobile phones, computers and microwave ovens. These can all aggravate negative Uranian symptoms.

○ We are all suffering from stimulation overload, so switch off your phone, computer and television and take a quiet walk in the country

○ If you are bored, frustrated or feeling trapped, do something about it before you attract a catastrophe

○ If you aren't being true to yourself, admit it now and take the first courageous steps to change

○ Feel free to do something crazy: dye your hair purple, go bungee-jumping or have a midnight picnic under a full summer Moon

○ Find a cause that you believe in and do something to make the world a better place

Aspects to Uranus (including transits)

Uranus–Sun
See page 34.

Uranus–Moon
See page 46.

Uranus–Mercury
See page 57.

Uranus–Venus
See page 67.

Uranus–Mars
See page 78.

Uranus–Jupiter
See page 87.

Uranus–Saturn
See page 96.

Uranus–Neptune

KEYWORDS: For the good of the whole

Since these are aspects formed between two generational planets, the effect on the individual is not so marked unless the two planets are predominant in the chart such as on one of the angles of involving other planets. Should this be the case, the individual would need to focus on altruistic social matters and pursuits since neither of these planets is concerned with the self. If this doesn't happen and too much focus is directed towards oneself and one's own interests, the Uranian energies could backfire in the form of stroke, or heart or breathing problems.

The key to keeping on the right side of these two planets is to dedicate oneself to trying to make society a better place.

HERBS AND SPICES: garlic, motherwort, valerian, vervain, yarrow

BACH FLOWERS: rock water, vervain, water violet

COLOUR: turquoise

AROMATHERAPY OILS: ginger, lavender, melissa, neroli, peppermint

VITAMINS AND MINERALS: copper, lecithin, magnesium, manganese, selenium

Uranus–Pluto

KEYWORD: Fanaticism

Another generational aspect, the effects of a Uranus–Pluto contact won't be particularly noticeable unless prominently placed or aspecting other personal planets. Should this be the case, problems may result from a fanatical and controversial nature, with the result that the nervous system could collapse leading to stroke or painful spasms. Accidents are also more likely with this combination of planets.

HERBS AND SPICES: angelica root, motherwort, skullcap, valerian, vervain

BACH FLOWERS: holly, rock rose, rock water, star of Bethlehem, vervain, vine, water violet

COLOURS: blue, green, lilac, turquoise, yellow

AROMATHERAPY OILS: clary sage, frankincense, ginger, neroli, patchouli, rosewood

VITAMINS AND MINERALS: magnesium, manganese, selenium, vitamin B complex

11

Neptune – The Stuff That Dreams Are Made Of

*'Dreams are illustrations … from the book your soul
is writing about you.'*
MARSHA NORMAN

As we move further out into the solar system and reach the penultimate planet, Neptune, nothing is quite what it seems anymore. This is where we enter the world of Alice in Wonderland. This is the stuff of which dreams are made and illusion is cast. While Neptune is a beautiful and spiritual planet embodying compassion and unconditional love, we don't really know where we stand with it. Its beauty and dreaminess can be as alluring as a full Moon reflected in a still lake, but ultimately it can be deceptive – it can make us see things that aren't really there.

We are all one

Neptune has no time for boundaries, limits and structures because such things separate and confine, while Neptune's desire is to be at one with everything – including the enemy. Such a philosophy can leave us wide open to attack and consequently Neptune often casts itself in the role of victim. Obviously this does not bode well for health, and astrologers see Neptune in the chart as a severely weakening and troublesome factor. It can be guilty of causing mysterious ailments, wrong diagnoses and illness that doesn't respond to obvious forms of treatment. With Neptune-related problems we are unlikely to be triumphant through conventional means; what's needed is something altogether different – a total integration of mind, body and spirit.

Physiological correspondences

Neptune governs the lymphatic system, the right brain function, the pineal gland, the appendix and the eyes. Its role within the body is that of absorption such as absorbing nutrients into the cells. Because of Neptune's weakening influence, it also has a definite effect upon the immune system and a prominent Neptune can lead to immunity disorders and problems of a psychological or emotional nature such as schizophrenia.

Immunity

We have already looked at the importance of Mars to the immune system, so why would Neptune which, let's face it, is the antithesis of Mars, being weak, vacillating and totally accepting, also have a role in our immunity? Well, while Neptune's role may not actually be to maintain our immune system, it can totally ruin it. And with an ever-increasing number of people succumbing to immunity disorders such as ME, AIDS, cancer and allergies, we perhaps need to ask why this is so. A clearer understanding of Neptune might help since it would seem to be the case that a great many of us are not expressing our Neptunes.

Neptune is first and foremost a spiritual planet – it seeks oneness with the universe and all living souls. Neptune has no time for goal-setting, striving and achieving, but if it did its goal would be unity of consciousness. It functions best when able to utilise its compassion and innate love for all beings. It's happy when it can inspire, uplift and heal others with its art, music or drama or its compassionate actions. It is Mother Theresa incarnate. It is the spiritual healer, the empathic counsellor, the visionary artist, the method actor and the meditating monk. It is totally harmless unless, of course, it sees no value within itself and then it begins to fall apart. Because Neptune (and Piscean) people don't have a strong identity – they're everyone and no one at the same time – they can often fall into victim mode and allow people to take advantage of or abuse them. Many Piscean and Neptune people are victims of abuse in one form or another and their biggest task is to develop inner strength and some kind of identity without losing any of their inherent compassion. A weak immune system then is often a reflection of a weak sense of self. If we don't know who we are, how can we differentiate between ourselves and others, and how can we separate the good germs from the bad?

This is what happens with allergic reactions; the immune system doesn't recognise that flower pollen or cat fur is totally harmless – it can't differentiate and so it reacts as it would to a genuine threat. With allergies there is also perhaps a sense that the world isn't safe and that everything is out to attack us – the Neptune victim mentality in operation again. In order to strengthen our immunity, we need to toughen up emotionally and mentally. We need to love ourselves and drop the guilt. We need to recognise that, while we are all connected, we are all individuals too and as such demand respect for who we are and the unique set of talents that we possess. Just as no two snowflakes are identical and no two birth charts are exactly the same, so too is every human unique. Neptunians need to remember this. When they do, they should find it easier to ward off disease.

We also need to bear in mind the colossal impact our thoughts and feelings have on our immune system. When down or depressed, we are far more likely to succumb to the bug doing the rounds than we are if we're happy and enthusiastic about life. Therefore, the 'what's the point' attitude commonly associated with Neptune needs to be replaced with a more positive outlook.

Addictions

If there's one thing Neptune can't abide, it's dreary, mundane reality. Neptune needs colour and would rather live in a fantasy world than face grey normality every day. Likewise, when the going gets tough and problems arise, Neptune will be the first to look for the escape route. For some born under Neptune's influence this means alcohol, for others it's drugs, but let's not forget that escapism and addictions come in a colourful array of choices including sleep, television, sex, sugar, caffeine, food and glamour. Art, music, acting and spiritual practices such as meditation are the healthier, more acceptable forms of escapism, though what the Neptune person is really seeking is an inspirational union with God or the cosmos. Creative and spiritual methods are the ideal ways for achieving this as we can really connect with our own spark of divinity only when we are either creating or when we are still and quiet enough to hear our own internal whispers.

Addictions represent a longing and since many of them facilitate an alteration in consciousness we can conclude that what is longed for is some kind of spiritual experience. Of course each addiction means something slightly different, but ultimately they express the need to escape a life that isn't completely fulfilling and they reflect an area of inner emptiness or pain. Many addictions reinforce the self-loathing and victim mentality since every addiction is a form of punishment of the self. Learning to love and respect ourselves as individuals is the first important step when dealing with any addiction – we are worth more than this abuse we are inflicting upon ourselves on a daily basis. When we have found the God within, life suddenly becomes the beautiful colourful experience that we always longed for, only we found it within instead of without, at the bottom of a bottle or in the toxic chemicals of the cigarette.

Mental and emotional disorders

While no one likes illness and disease, we are at least more comfortable when we can put a label on it and identify it (often wrongly) as something that came from outside of us. Not so with mental and emotional disorders. For many people these are frightening – largely because we don't understand them let alone know how to deal with them. Perhaps more importantly, we fear such disorders because they are beyond our control and are a reminder that the same could happen to us. We too could lose control of our rational selves and suffer from a nervous breakdown, depression, Alzheimer's or a bout of schizophrenia. What's most frightening of all, though, is that these conditions facilitate the release of our dark side. Everything that we've tried to deny, suppress or sweep under the carpet suddenly becomes too much and erupts like a volcano spilling its ugly contents for all the world to see. Much easier, then, to try and keep the lid on the dark forces bubbling away underneath with a plentiful supply of drugs. Trying is the operative word here because sooner or later the drugs wear off and the symptoms burst forth.

Neptune corresponds to the 6th and 7th chakras, which deal with intuition, right-brain function and spirituality. To deny this vitally important part of human beings is asking for trouble. Neptune likes to project the illusion of peace and beauty, but when it lets rip it really goes to town, and if suppressed for long enough it will throw a tantrum in the style of a 'lovey' actor who has been overlooked for too long. Don't forget that Neptune is Poseidon, God of the sea, and the sea can get pretty stormy at times. So what's needed for good mental health is a combination of accepting our whole selves, not confining ourselves to being one kind of person – usually the straightforward, moral, upright person projecting the image of a closet devoid of skeletons – and developing our awareness that we are not separate. The single snowflake's beauty is matched only by the blanket of snow draped over the rolling fields.

Living in harmony with Neptune – intuition, creativity and soulfulness

As we have discovered, not expressing our Neptune in a healthy way can have devastating repercussions on our health. If we over-identify with Neptune in the form of feeling victimised, being unsure of who we are or why we're here, or living in a fantasy world and unable to face up to reality, we are leaving ourselves wide open to attack – both psychologically and physically in the form of allergies, infections and auto-immune diseases such as lupus and ME. If we under-identify with Neptune and consider ourselves totally separate from others and exist in a cold logical world devoid of beauty and magic, we may succumb to similar problems but are more liable to experience the psycho-emotional disorders where the left brain bows out and takes a back seat to the antics of the right brain. This could take the form of delusions, hallucinations, schizophrenia and mental or emotional breakdowns. We need to find the balance between soulful compassion and a healthy sense of self.

Soul work

It is essential to remember that Neptune is first and foremost a planet dealing with the spiritual, intuitive side of life, and so any Neptunian illness is a sign that we need to do a little soul work. This can be very difficult for those left-brained people who can't even accept the concept of the soul, never mind try to reconnect with it. The same holds true for the escapist drug addicts and alcoholics. They may be heading in the right direction – towards non-separation and humility – but have found themselves on the wrong path, a little like knowing where you want to be heading but putting the wrong fuel in the car so you end up going nowhere. We all need to acknowledge that we are all connected and therefore part of the whole and that whenever we harm another we are ultimately hurting ourselves. This is why developing compassion is perhaps more important than delving into past lives, reading the tarot cards, dowsing or communicating with guardian angels and entities from other planets. These pursuits are all welcomed by Neptune and can be helpful in developing our connection with our higher self, but so long as we are striving to become gentle, elegant spirits, displaying loving kindness and care towards all living beings, Neptune will be more than happy.

Art, magic and beauty

If there's one thing Neptune loves it's a bit of colourful fantasy. We have Neptune to thank for our fairy tales, enchanted forests, unicorns, elves, angels and goblins. Neptune lights up our lives and makes us believe that anything is possible. Have you ever sat and watched a rainbow? It's such a magical part of life on earth and yet we only get to glimpse its beauty occasionally. Neptune loves casting rainbows and perpetuating the belief that there's a pot of gold at the end. And why not? We all need to dream and hope, otherwise life becomes stale and meaningless. The truth is, we don't really know what's possible, least of all within ourselves. So pick up the paintbrush or the camera, join the actors' workshop, write that fantasy novel, dare to believe that there is a guardian angel standing at your shoulder and that there are nature spirits dancing on the cherry blossom tree at the bottom of your garden. Who cares whether it's real or not? We can't prove beauty or define magic. Life is merely a dream from which we'll wake anyway. Create your own rainbows and your heart will sing all the louder for it.

Your Neptune is out of balance when:

- O You can't get through the day without a drink, smoke, daily dose of soaps or whatever else you can't live without

- O You repeatedly let people take advantage of you

- O You cast yourself in the role of victim or martyr

- O You find it very difficult to say no

- O You don't know where you're going

- O Other people deceive you, or you deceive others

- O You're very much into going with the flow but end up going nowhere

To increase the strength of your Neptune and your immunity:

○ Create a sacred space where you can be alone

○ Learn to meditate

○ Develop your sense of self: you're unique and deserve to be happy by virtue of that fact

○ Let go of guilt and self-loathing: you are only doing the best you can

○ If you feel you're a bit of a pushover and if people take advantage of you, develop your assertiveness – do a course, read the books, listen to the tapes

○ Instead of drowning your sorrows in a bottle or running away from your problems, face up to them and take the necessary action

○ Get to know yourself – when you do you'll have a clearer idea of what you were put here for

○ Don't think that to accept your 'shadow' side is unspiritual: we all need to earn money, we all have physical desires and we all have characteristics we're not proud of – it's simply part of being human

○ Pay attention to your intuition – the more you do the stronger it will become

○ Go with the flow: sometimes the universe knows better than we do which direction to go in

○ If a problem is getting you down, hand it over to a higher power and ask for help

○ Let yourself be uplifted more often with inspirational art, prose or music

○ Don't let life become too grey: escape every so often into books, films, art or whatever transports you into another world

Aspects to Neptune (including transits)

Neptune–Sun
See page 35.

Neptune–Moon
See page 46.

Neptune–Mercury
See page 57.

Neptune–Venus
See page 68.

Neptune–Mars
See page 79.

Neptune–Jupiter
See page 88.

Neptune–Saturn
See page 97.

Neptune–Uranus
See page 106.

Neptune–Pluto

KEYWORD: Surrender

Since this is a generational aspect, affecting very large numbers of people, its influence on the individual is far less marked than it is for the generation, and so its effect on health is negligible. The hard aspects may incline one towards resignation and a lack of will to fight so, unless there are other more motivational factors in the chart, giving up and surrendering are the biggest problems here. For this reason, the remedies most suited are those that give a fighting spirit and a will to carry on.

HERBS AND SPICES: motherwort, nettle, wild oat

BACH FLOWERS: hornbeam, wild rose

COLOUR: red

AROMATHERAPY OILS: basil, black pepper, clove, ginger, pine

12

Pluto – The Darkest Hour Before the Dawn

'I have a little shadow that goes in and out with me,
And what can be the use of him is more than I can see.'
ROBERT LOUIS STEVENSON

What use indeed? What's the point of our shadow if not to cause us, and others, a whole lot of bother? What is our shadow anyway? A few unpleasant characteristics that we mask with a pleasant smile so as to fool others into thinking we're always a nice, good person? Or does it go deeper than that? Is it actually a whole other world that we'd rather not even admit might possibly exist? Welcome to Pluto.

The long dark night of the soul

We had a taste of life in other worlds as we travelled through Neptune's murky oceanic depths and languid lagoons. But with Pluto we venture even further below, into the bowels of the earth no less, but here there is no ambiguity of atmosphere; it is all dark – intensely so. Most people don't want to have anything to do with Pluto, understandably, because he is Pandora's box, the devil and hell all rolled into one. It's not likely to be a pretty sight wherever he lurks in our personalities and whichever domain he occupies in our chart is the one we desperately try and keep a lid on – unless, that is, we're either very brave, very foolish or a combination of both. However Pluto, like Saturn, is not one for letting us avoid our lessons – or in Pluto's case, our shadow side – and sooner or later we have to confront that which we've suppressed or denied for too long. The longer it takes to do this, the more problems we set up for ourselves, and one of the consequences of an ignored Pluto can be serious, life-threatening health problems.

Pluto and serious disease

Pluto – along with Saturn – is likely to play a large part in the manifestation of cancer, as our suppressed inner demons – fear, hurt, resentment, hatred and anger – turn nasty and cause untold damage. Whereas Saturn mainly reflects our fears and insecurities, Pluto gathers all our negative painful experiences and stuffs them in a black box labelled 'Danger – toxic waste!'. The consequence of dragging such a hefty load around with us all the time – besides the possibility of illness – is a reluctance to take on any more experiences, and so we close off to life. We certainly don't want to have to endure any more of what we've crammed in the box, thank you very much. But nobody forces us to carry our garbage round with us, we are always free to let it go. And this is ultimately what Pluto expects of us – to let go of our old selves and transform into something new.

Physiological correspondences

Since Pluto governs the dark side of human life, it's hardly surprising that the areas of the body he represents are those we'd rather not discuss in polite company. The eliminatory and reproductive organs along with the genitals are Pluto's domain and any difficulties that we have in letting go emotionally will be reflected in problems here such as cystitis, constipation, piles (haemorrhoids) or, far more seriously, bowel cancer. Childbirth is also a Plutonic experience, reflecting the intense life and death struggle and the transformative process of a new life emerging. Abscesses, boils, malignant tumours and poisonous bites are Plutonic in nature. Ultimately, Pluto's task within the body and mind is to purify, cleanse and transform.

Elimination – the need to let go

Every living creature consumes food, extracts the nutrients and expels the waste. Holding on to waste matter, as in constipation, becomes toxic to the body and ultimately very dangerous. This inability to let go is reflective of a lack of trust, a fear that everything won't be okay if controls are released. Constipation is a way of having power or control over uncertain situations. It is very difficult to have a bowel movement if we're feeling stressed, hurried or nervous. Regular bouts of constipation are an indication that we need to slow down, relax our controls and let go of all that is no longer useful for us.

Piles occur when we strain to expel our waste matter and such straining implies a dilemma between letting go and maintaining control. Elimination, like all Plutonic processes, requires a period of gestation and cannot be hurried or forced. With haemorrhoids we may be trying to force an issue or get rid of something before the time is right. This could mean that we haven't fully completed, absorbed or accepted something, whether it be a situation, a relationship, a project or a lesson that we need to learn.

Bowel problems are becoming increasingly common. Irritable bowel syndrome (IBS) is a frequent complaint and incidences of bowel cancer are rising. There's no doubt that our diet and lifestyle play a huge part in these problems – IBS in particular is related to a stressful, hurried pace of life and a poor diet – but when we fail to take adequate care of ourselves it is usually a reflection that there is something amiss on an inner level. Perhaps these bowel complaints are reflective of the increasing uncertainty that we face in the modern world. The dislocation of the family unit – once the emotional anchor in our lives – is bound to have a destabilising effect on people. There are no longer any jobs for life, and this is very disconcerting for those who need physical and emotional security. We live in a time of huge change and increasing chaos. We cannot really depend on anything because just as we get used to something it changes.

I make no judgement whether this is a good thing or not. There is a positive element to every condition and, while we've never seen so much uncertainty and such rapid change, we've also never had so much opportunity. We are freer and more able to achieve than ever before. The answer, it would seem, is not to bemoan the state of the world but to let go of our attachment to people, places and situations. We need to find inner security because we're not going to find it externally in the world. We need to trust in a higher power, to recognise that the universe will guide us accordingly and that everything will work out for our highest good. We are rather like corks on a turbulent ocean at the moment. We can either struggle against the waves or relax and enjoy the journey.

Reproduction and sexuality

Pluto is not the easiest planet to get along with since he demands an awful lot from us – namely the willingness to plunge into the darkest experiences of life and come out the other side a little different from when we went in. Pluto requires us to die and transform – not a literal death, obviously, but a symbolic one. In order to do this we need to surrender, yet if we're afraid of letting go we may experience sexual or reproductive disorders.

This isn't just about letting go of the fear of what might happen if we open up and trust someone; it's also about letting go of painful memories. For people who have been abused, a healthy sex life is much more difficult than for those who haven't. The consequential feelings of guilt, shame, self-loathing and disgust can completely close down the natural sexual responses and the result can be frigidity and impotence, problem periods and cervical cancer. Of course, we may not even have to endure abuse to feel guilt and shame since many people are brought up to feel that sex is bad or something that must only be experienced to facilitate reproduction. Pornography makes it difficult for people to equate sex with love and religion frowns on any form of sexual 'deviancy.' Consequently many of us are walking around with a host of sexual hang-ups, so it's hardly surprising that disorders of the sexual and reproductive organs are on the increase.

Pluto and intimacy

We may also have sexual difficulties if we fear sharing ourselves with another. It can be rather frightening to open yourself up totally to another person and it often takes real courage to experience and accept such feelings of vulnerability. Far easier to have a close, safe, non-sexual relationship with a marriage partner or good friend, and sex with someone else with whom we don't have a strong emotional connection.

Rectifying problems within this very complex area can be difficult and may take time. However, it is worth bearing in mind that most problems in this area are connected to fear of being hurt or abused and this can be seen in the chart via Pluto's position as he is the planet of control par excellence. Reproductive difficulties such as PMS, amenorrhoea, cervical disorders and ovarian cysts are often a resistance to going with the flow or a dislike of being female. If we are uneasy with being a woman and are too controlling we may well have problems with our monthly flow. Regular pain-free periods require a surrendering to the whole process of being female and a willingness to be under the control of nature's cycles. We reject the most female aspect of ourselves because we find the modern complications of what it means to be a woman too confusing. Should we have a successful career or should we be a full-time mother? How much aggression and power are we allowed to display? And so on.

Ultimately, we need to be trust ourselves on this one and not be dictated to by what is the current trend within society. If you feel the urge to be a full-time mother and finances permit – go ahead. If, on the other hand, you'd be bored to death and need a career, don't let anyone else pile on the guilt.

Living in harmony with Pluto – transformation, letting go and forgiveness

The first thing you'll need to live in peace with Pluto is courage. You'll never live in harmony with him if you only ever live life on the surface or are afraid to dig deep within yourself. If there is a situation in your life that has run its course, whether it be a job, a relationship, or a phase of life such as the menopause or bereavement, it's time to muster up some courage, do what you need to do, grieve and move on. The same applies to your beliefs and attitudes that may not always be healthy. Confront your shadow – listen to its grievances, its resentments and frustrations. Acknowledge that you might be angry, hurt, guilty, or whatever. Accept that there might be a part of you that never sees the light of day – a part full of longing, but because of the upset or changes it might entail is kept hidden in the basement. This isn't to suggest that we should all forget our morals and behave in ways that would make the devil's hair curl, but we do at least need to acknowledge that these parts of us exist, and then find sensible, healthy ways in which to deal with them. To deny human impulses and try to pretend that we're all saint-like is asking for trouble.

Transformation

The point of transformation is always preceded by immense struggle. All birth requires a struggle – the baby chick has to force its way out of the shell just as the butterfly has to push out of its chrysalis and emerge into the world a far more liberated and arguably more beautiful creature than it was before. And this is why Pluto resides at the end of the planetary spectrum; we have reached the end and must prepare to die and be reborn. All serious illness requires an element of transformation – we must let go of the old attitudes, lifestyles or beliefs that have led to the manifestation of the particular illness. This can feel like a part of us is dying. Perhaps we overly identified with being a wife and mother, and so when the husband leaves for a younger woman or our children leave home, we are left with a sense of anger and bitterness because our whole sense of self has fallen apart. Or maybe we identified ourselves with our career, we gained our sense of worth from being a successful person, so when suddenly we are made redundant or we stop succeeding the resulting stress and confusion can lead to illness.

At these points in our lives we need to expand our sense of who we are while simultaneously letting go of anger, blame, guilt or any other destructive emotion that has taken residence as a result of the stressful situation. Likewise when a parent, child, sibling or spouse dies, we also lose a part of ourselves – we're no longer a husband, a father, a sister or a child. If we are willing we can learn an awful lot from our illnesses and the only way in which we will recover our health is to have the courage to look at where we might be going wrong and be willing to change.

Letting go and forgiving

The process of letting go is similar to that of transformation in that we need to release our old self and sit through the intensely painful process of being in the void – that black space of nothingness when we've lost something dear to us and don't know where to go or what to do next. But we can also practise letting go on a day-to-day basis with the little things in life. We can let go of the need to be right in an argument. When another driver is rude and cuts us up we can choose to let it go and give the benefit of the doubt – perhaps he or she is having a bad day. We can let go of the need to get even with the awkward neighbour or the ex-lover who betrayed us. Revenge is one of the hallmarks of Pluto, but this kind of response to being hurt or attacked is more damaging to the plotter than to anyone else. The kind of black thoughts and negative emotions we entertain when in a vengeful frame of mind are perhaps the most self-destructive of all. And if we do act out our vengeful fantasies, we only create a vicious circle that will be perpetuated until one or other party is big enough to let it go. It's also worth remembering that we are karmically tied to anyone for whom we have strong feelings, whether they be loving feelings or hateful ones. So it's not just better for your health and peace of mind to forgive, but you'll also create a future incarnation where you won't be drawn into the same destructive situations with the same people again.

Going with the flow

Wherever Pluto (or Scorpio) sits in our charts will be the place where we try and have complete power and maintain total control. If we are a Plutonic person with several planets in Scorpio or in the 8th house, or with Pluto in a prominent position or aspecting the Sun or Mars, we run the risk of doing ourselves more harm than good with our controlling, vengeful nature. Pluto is the most destructive of all the planets – he rules death, after all – and it's all too easy for the immense power of Pluto to backfire and destroy the self. We can get caught up in destructive or cruel power games where the need to come out on top is vital. It won't do us any harm to lose once or twice, for to pass Pluto's test we must be able to relinquish our external powers. Perhaps this means holding up your hands and saying 'I don't know', or maybe it means being able to lose with a peaceful heart a contest, whether it be related to love, sport or career. Maybe it's about throwing yourself hook, line and sinker into a relationship and experiencing the vulnerability that goes with it. Perhaps it means being able to face death – your own or other people's. Or maybe your personal Pluto task is to look within and confront your own inner demons.

Whatever Pluto asks of you – and it will be the hardest thing you'll ever have to do – it's worth mustering the courage to face him, because a successfully mastered Pluto is like the butterfly emerging from the chrysalis. You won't be able to go back to your previous state, but with your new-found liberation you're unlikely to want to.

Your Pluto is out of balance when:

○ You're still plotting revenge for something that happened years ago

○ You're afraid or unable to trust another in case he or she hurts you

○ You're unable to let go of the hurt or anger you feel for events that happened in childhood

○ You enjoy (or would enjoy) being in a position of power

○ Your anger can be so intense that it frightens you

○ You can be self-destructive – you'd rather destroy yourself than let someone else have victory over you

To increase the strength of your Pluto and the health of your bowel and reproductive organs:

○ Learn to let go – the single most important Pluto lesson

○ Become less controlling – allow yourself to be carried along from time to time

○ Admit to your vulnerability: we're all afraid of getting hurt, but to fully experience life in all its glory requires us to take the odd chance with our feelings

○ Have something worthwhile to channel your energies into – a career, a goal, a project, anything: Pluto needs something to focus on, otherwise he will become self-destructive

○ Be prepared to shed your skin every so often and allow the new you to emerge

○ Go with the flow and be more accepting of what life throws at you

○ Don't try to hold on to the past: when autumn comes the trees don't struggle to hold on to their leaves – they willingly release them knowing that they're participating in the natural ebb and flow of things and that new leaves will come

○ Try not to judge periods of pain and loss as bad: we can learn a lot from these times and grow stronger as a result

○ Have regular clearouts: Pluto thrives on cleansing and purifying so take the opportunity to cleanse and detoxify, not just your physical self and your home but also your emotions, beliefs and attitudes. Let go of all the old baggage.

○ Watch out for imbalances of power within your relationships: make sure you are an equal – neither inferior nor superior

○ Keeping secrets or valuable information from others is a sign of a power complex. Reverse the situation – would you be happy being kept in the dark?

○ Watch out for manipulation – your own or other people's. Trying to push others to do what you want is an abuse of power and reveals hidden insecurities.

Aspects to Pluto (including transits)

Pluto–Sun
See page 35.

Pluto–Moon
See page 47.

Pluto–Mercury
See page 58.

Pluto–Venus
See page 69.

Pluto–Mars
See page 79.

Pluto–Jupiter
See page 88.

Pluto–Saturn
See page 98.

Pluto–Uranus
See page 106.

Pluto–Neptune
See page 115.

13

Transits – The Times of Your Life

'It was the best of times, it was the worst of times.'
CHARLES DICKENS, *A TALE OF TWO CITIES*

Have you ever noticed how life seems to be trundling along reasonably okay, when suddenly, bang – everything's turned upside-down? Say hello to your Uranus transit. Or you wake up one morning and have to admit that you're bored, depressed and generally fed up. Chances are that Saturn has decided to pay you a visit. Or perhaps you suffer a profound loss and you swear life will never be the same again. You've just made Pluto's acquaintance.

We might be familiar with the planets in our own chart and have an idea of how they reveal elements of our character and physical weaknesses, but it's only when these same planets move round our chart and activate other planets that we really feel and begin to understand their energies. This is the nature of a transit, roughly translated as a planetary movement.

As we've discovered, each planet governs a different area of life or being, and when a planet makes its presence felt it is asking you to adopt these qualities into your life. This is often difficult, especially if the planet's qualities are at odds with your basic nature. For example if you're basically Saturnian in nature (ordered, nine-to-five job, living to routines, fearful of change) you'll most probably struggle when unpredictable Uranus bursts on to the scene and wants to liven things up a bit. This can cause intense stress, which in turn can lead to ill health or accidents. This is why transits are notorious for provoking health complaints, so it makes sense to keep your eye on the planetary movements in relation to your chart so that you can be well prepared. Knowing which therapies and remedies work with which planet will be invaluable to you while going through that particular planetary transit. When you know what a planet requires of you, you can work with it and make its lessons much easier to learn.

Working out your transits

After reading through this chapter you may be keen to discover which transits you're undergoing at the moment so that you can work with them. The standard way is to have an astrologer work out your current transits, or if you have a chart you can work it out yourself by placing the current positions of the planets on to your own chart. Although a detailed analysis of transits is beyond the scope of this book, you can gain a rough idea by keeping your eye on the movements of the planets and having a few basic rules in mind.

The most notable times are when a planet moves through your Sun, Moon or Rising Sign, or when a planet returns to its natal position. For example, Saturn takes 28 years to go round the zodiac, so we all have our Saturn returns between 28 and 30 – a time when we're learning about responsibility and making necessary changes to our lives.

Difficult times are when an outer planet – Saturn, Uranus, Neptune or Pluto – moves through your sign, or the sign opposite or square to yours. At the time of writing Saturn is in Gemini. Therefore all Geminis will have been experiencing Saturn's lessons, through restriction, greater responsibility or making changes to alleviate discontent. Those born under Sagittarius – the sign opposite to Gemini – would have been feeling his weight too, most notably in their relationships. The signs square to Gemini are Pisces and Virgo, so these signs would also have had certain stresses and challenges to deal with. If you want to know when your good times will be, check out Jupiter's movements and when he goes through your sign you can expect a year of good fortune and opportunity.

Obviously this is a very simplified approach to transits, but it gives you an idea if you're new to this area of astrology. Now let's look at the planets in action.

Saturn transits

An approaching Saturn transit is enough to turn most astrologers' knees to jelly. Even though we know that when he leaves we'll be stronger and wiser, we still don't much relish his presence in our lives, especially if we're Uranian in nature, which most astrologers are. However, problems arise under a Saturn transit only when we haven't got our house in order. He is both the hard taskmaster and the wise teacher of the zodiac. He is firm but fair and represents our deepest fears, blocks and insecurities. The areas of life where we can't seem to have what we want are Saturn's domain, but if we are prepared to work hard and be honest with ourselves, he will help us achieve that which appears so elusive.

During a Saturn transit, you may be faced with these fears and blockages as he reminds you of the pact you made with yourself long ago to work on these aspects of yourself. The good news is that your Saturn transit will help you to make real progress in these blocked areas – if, of course, you put in the necessary effort.

Saturn's approach

You're unlikely to notice Saturn creeping up on you. His approach is slow, measured and unobtrusive. He doesn't need a big fanfare to signal his arrival, unlike Uranus who would bring a circus to town (but minus the animals because that would be cruel). Your first clue is a heavy presence followed by fatigue or a vague sense of discontent. At this point you'd better start checking that your spiritual accounts are in order. If they are sadly lacking you need to begin balancing any karmic debts quickly and start taking greater responsibility for what happens in your life. However, if you were caught napping and woke to find Saturn staring sternly at your imbalanced accounts, there would be nothing for it but to accept your admonishment and learn from it.

Illness and symptoms

Physical illness or depression during a Saturn transit is often a sign that we are discontented about something, and probably have been for quite some time. Saturn conditions are long term and often linked to rigidity of the mind, so we might expect stiff muscles, aching limbs and joints (at the mild end) or the onset of arthritis or severe back problems. Broken bones, dislocations and teeth, skin and hair problems, along with a lowered sex drive can all appear during a Saturn transit.

Recognising a Saturn transit:

○ Feeling discontented, frustrated or fed up with the way things are

○ Coming up against blocks, feeling thwarted

○ Feelings of restriction and limitation

○ Feeling run down and physically drained

○ Feeling low or depressed

○ Currently feeling that life is hard or difficult

○ Noticing that you don't laugh or have as much fun as you used to

○ Feeling or having to be more serious and responsible

○ Feeling under immense pressure to change the situation you're in but not knowing how

○ Knowing that there are things you need to do to improve your life

To work with your Saturn transit:

○ Face up to and deal with your responsibilities

○ Eat warming spices such as ginger to increase your energy and improve poor digestion

○ Be more structured and organised

○ Operate with honesty and integrity

○ Do things that bring you joy and make you laugh

○ Don't be too hard on yourself

○ Be honest about what's not working in your life

○ Acknowledge your fears and insecurities

○ Take regular exercise to stimulate a sluggish system and increase feelings of optimism

○ Take up dance, tai-chi, yoga, massage or the Alexander technique – they are all excellent methods for loosening up stiffness in both body and mind

○ Use the Bach flower remedies aspen, larch and mimulus – all Saturnian remedies to help alleviate fear and insecurities

○ Wear or use the colour orange, which helps balance Saturn's grey, heavy energy

○ Try to become more flexible and less resistant to change or to other people

Uranus transits

Uranus is the planet of change and revolution. He acts suddenly and without any warning and so can be very destabilising. Where Uranus goes, nothing stays the same for very long. His purpose is to liberate us from that which has become stale and boring. He's the planet that can make you feel like a teenager again when you're going through your mid-life crisis and there's the general feeling that anything could happen. On the downside, he can upset the apple cart when you'd just got used to security and stability, but even when he brings an unpleasant shock there is always method behind his madness. A Uranus transit will leave you feeling alive and refreshed.

Uranus's approach

You might expect that when Uranus comes to town his entry will be dramatic, unusual, totally unexpected and in keeping with his unpredictable nature. You may look at other spectators' bemused: 'I didn't invite him. Did you?'. Well, actually you probably did, and not only did you invite him but he'll also have given you some warnings of his arrival, only you chose to ignore them.

Dealing with a Uranian transit can be either extremely difficult or exciting and liberating, depending on how you look at it. At least with Saturn we know where we are, we know what to expect and how to deal with it. Uranus by stark contrast is like the court jester, The Joker in *Batman,* the clown at a kids' party or the rebellious teenager's birthday bash. Anything could, and probably will, happen.

Illness and symptoms

When we suffer physically as a result of a Uranus transit it's usually because we've been ignoring the fact that something needs to change. This is especially true if we have an accident. Perhaps we are struggling against what life has in mind for us, clinging to the wreckage of some aspect of our life that sorely needs to change. The resulting pressure of knowing we need to make a change but dare not can be very stressful. We're therefore much more likely to attract an accident under a Uranus transit, which signals that we need to take some time out to look at what we're doing and where we're going.

Physical symptoms of a Uranian transit include palpitations, tremors and twitches, mental instability, anxiety, disorders of the nervous system, and injuries sustained through accidents.

Recognising a Uranus transit:

- Electrical items acting oddly around you
- Feeling you're going crazy
- Acting unpredictably
- Yearning for change or freedom
- Feeling bored and wanting to change things
- Finding it very difficult to relax
- Sudden unpredictable or shocking events
- Getting glimpses of other dimensions or other 'weird' things happening
- Accidents or mishaps – minor to major
- Panic attacks or palpitations
- Mental instability and nervousness
- Muscular cramps, twitches or tics
- Sudden bursts of energy

To work with your Uranus transit:

- Try to spend as much time in nature as you can
- Practice yoga, tai-chi or meditation to help ground and calm you
- Take gentle exercise such as walking, hiking, gardening etc.
- Take hot baths with sea salt
- Use relaxing herbs such as chamomile and valerian to help keep you calm
- Try to keep to regular eating and sleeping patterns
- If you feel like throwing caution to the wind, consider the consequences of your actions
- Try not to resist any changes thrust upon you – just go with the flow

○ Avoid all stimulants such as coffee, chocolate, alcohol, cigarettes, tea and artificial additives, and appliances that can interfere with the brain and nervous system such as mobile phones, PCs and microwaves

○ Use aromatherapy oils such as chamomile, lavender, neroli, patchouli and sandalwood to help calm and ground you

○ Use the Bach flower remedies rock rose and star of Bethlehem to help deal with any shocks; walnut will help you adjust to change; vervain and impatiens will help to calm, relieving tension and anxiety

Neptune transits

Neptune is the planet that connects each and every one of us to God. It has a deeply spiritual essence and blesses us with ideals, visions, artistic talent and the blissful state of spiritual union that comes with connecting to your higher self. Neptune has no time for the material life, controls, barriers and separation for it knows that we are all one. When Neptune touches you on its travels, it is urging you to go within and look at what's really important. If you can do this, real peace and contentment will be yours.

Neptune's approach

If you didn't notice Saturn creeping up on you, then you've no chance with Neptune, such is the subtlety of its movements. Whereas Uranus is likely to whack you over the head, Neptune will weave itself into your dreams and float in the background of your consciousness, creating a sense of confusion or vagueness. Neptune is like mist rolling over moors: you can't touch, hear or smell it, but it's enough to disorientate you so much you end up going nowhere. Forgetfulness, tiredness and lethargy along with feeling spaced out and not really knowing who you are or where you're going signal that Neptune has well and truly arrived and wants you to reassess a few things.

Illness and symptoms

Neptune symptoms are notoriously vague and difficult to understand and diagnose. Consequently, it's worth getting a second or third opinion on any diagnosis when under Neptune's influence, especially when it involves surgery. Actually, under a Neptune transit we'd probably do better going for a natural approach to healing as the removal of any organ (unless it is to treat a life threatening condition) is unlikely to address the problem that Neptune is asking us to answer. Any disease or symptom under a Neptune transit is usually asking us to take a more spiritual approach to life. If we have previously been very competitive, controlling, successful in a material sense or very left-brained and logical, a change of attitude may bring remarkable improvements.

Neptune symptoms include tiredness, dizziness, fainting, suicidal feelings, ME, candida (thrush), allergies, intolerances, emotional breakdowns, leaky gut and auto-immunity problems. Neptune disorders are characterised by feelings of weakness and tiredness along with confusion, vagueness or an inability to carry on. Such feelings usually hint at the need to surrender and let go of the need to be the tough one always in control.

Recognising a Neptune transit:

- Forgetfulness, confusion or feeling spaced out

- A desire to escape through drink, drugs, food, television, sex or sleep

- A desire to connect with your Higher self/God

- A need for romance

- An increase in your intuition or psychic ability

- Vague, hard to diagnose ailments or illnesses that don't respond to treatment

- Feelings of futility or lack of drive and motivation

- Life not going how you want it to, feeling like you're losing your grip

- Misunderstandings or indecision

- Looking at where you want to be and what you want to do with your life

- Feeling tired, lazy or weak

- Feeling more creative than usual

- Losing your sense of identity, not being sure who you are any more

To work with your Neptune transit:

○ Allow plenty of time to relax and just be

○ Trust your intuition not your logic – allow yourself to be guided by your inner voice

○ Keep a dream diary and take note of what your dreams are telling you

○ Develop your creativity, take up an artistic hobby, or simply dance and sing

○ Visit the cinema or art galleries, or take up swimming and meditation

○ Visualise what you want to happen

○ Go with the flow and relax your controls on life; trying to control life under a Neptune transit will fail

○ Try the Bach flower remedies wild oat to give clarity with direction, and wild rose to counter apathy

○ Join a group that explores spiritual, new age and/or mystical matters

○ Practise unconditional love – towards both others and yourself

○ Try not to analyse the situation or problem – simply let go and let God

Pluto transits

If you thought the previous transits were tough you ain't seen nothing yet!

A Pluto transit is perhaps the hardest of all because it can literally destroy everything and you can feel as though you are dying. But, as with all endings, a new beginning is in sight and Pluto asks you to purge yourself of all that no longer serves you – whether it be a real circumstance such as a tired relationship or, more commonly, an emotional wound that needs to be brought to the surface and healed.

Pluto's approach

Pluto doesn't really have an approach, though we can sometimes sense his nearness when we know that a long-term situation must come to an end. It's perhaps like having a dark shadow hovering over your shoulder. If word does get round that he's on his way, you'll be left standing in a ghost town – nobody wants to be around when death rides in.

Illness and symptoms

All Pluto's illnesses, regardless of whether it's an abscess or cancer, signal the need for cleansing and transformation. Pluto is heavily into detoxing, but remember that we need to detox our minds and hearts as well as our bodies. We can do this by choosing to let go of all our past pains and forgive those who have hurt us. If forgiveness seems impossible, bear in mind that the only person who is suffering by holding on to a grudge is you.

An illness under a Pluto transit is a clear signal that some aspect of ourselves or our lives needs to be purified and transformed. A painful situation that can't be transformed may need to be brought to an end so that we can move on and begin again. Sometimes, though, as in the case of a death, we have no control over the situation and we have to accept and face up to what's happened. With death, we need to grieve until there's nothing left to come out. The worst thing we can do is suppress or deny it, because it will catch up with us at a later date and erupt like a volcano.

Pluto symptoms include all forms of poison such as abscesses, appendicitis and insect bites and anything that rises to the surface such as skin problems (acne, eczema etc.) and vomiting. Life-threatening diseases are a severe wake-up call, reminding us that we must undergo a serious transformation whether it be within our lifestyle or our beliefs and attitudes. If we heed Pluto's lesson, we will emerge so much stronger and wiser than we were before.

Recognising a Pluto transit:

- Witnessing traumatic endings, such as deaths or the end of a relationship or job

- Feelings of despair – feeling like you can't go on

- Seeing your life being transformed around you

- Depression – light to severe

- Going through hell

- Compulsive, addictive, obsessive behaviour – your own or someone else's

- Having fears and phobias and feeling powerful emotions

- Feeling out of control along with extreme highs and lows

- Passionate relationships or sexual awakenings

- Vengeful thoughts or feelings – you want to get back at whoever has hurt you

- Issues of power: are you abusing it or allowing yourself to be abused?

To work with your Pluto transit:

○ Have regular periods of detoxification – eat healthy, natural food and drink lots of water

○ Practise yoga, tai-chi or meditation to help ground and calm you

○ Try to let go – struggling against the problem will only make things worse

○ Take time out to nurture and care for yourself

○ Try counselling or psychotherapy to help you through this difficult time

○ Use cleansing herbs such as dandelion root to help keep your body healthy

○ Avoid all addictive stimulants such as coffee, chocolate, alcohol, drugs and cigarettes

○ Use Bach flower remedies: try holly for rage, jealousy and hate and sweet chestnut for anguish and despair

○ The homoeopathic remedies nat mur and staphysagria are good at releasing deeply buried emotions, but consult a practitioner to determine the strength of potency required

○ Explore your emotions and don't be afraid to show your feelings

Taking transits in your stride

Obviously, this is looking at the darker implications of the transits of the outer planets, and the important thing to remember is that it doesn't necessarily have to be difficult. So much depends upon you as an individual and how you deal with the energies of the planets. A lot also depends on how much inner work you've done and if you've risen to meet the challenges of the tricky aspects within your own natal chart. If you have, then when these natal aspects are triggered by a transit you should emerge relatively unscathed. Saturn *can* conjunct your Moon and not leave you feeling as tearful and depressed as you'd expect, but only if everything's healthy in that domain. The planets are never unfair and they don't cause problems just for the sake of it – there is always method behind their madness. A Saturn transit will teach you the importance of responsibility – something you're not likely to appreciate at the time if you've only ever been concerned with having a good time, but which in later years you'll look back on with gratitude.

So with this in mind, you can arm yourself with your trusty ephemeris and greet your transits with open arms, knowing that they will teach you whatever you need to learn. And if no lesson is needed, it will just be business as usual.

14

Creating Health and Well-being

'Real health is happiness, and a happiness so easy
of attainment because it is happiness in small
things: doing the things we really love to do, being
with the people that we truly like.'
EDWARD BACH, *Free Thyself*

So now that we have seen how our mental and emotional states can create illness, how do we find the cure? What is needed to balance out our stressful inner states? Well, a lot depends upon the condition and the person, though we can usually sum up the ideal therapy in one word – change. If we always do what we've always done, we'll always get what we always got, and the same holds true for illness. If we have consistently high blood pressure we need to look at why this is and begin changing our emotional responses to everyday situations before it becomes more serious. Even frequent bouts of the common cold can be a signal to slow down and take greater care of ourselves. Our bodies are constantly trying to communicate with us via discomfort and aches and pains. It's up to us whether we choose to listen or not.

Illness is a plea for change and, while astrology may be a wonderful and enlightening tool for diagnosing problems and understanding people, we usually need to bring in various other healing techniques in order to support people through the necessary changes. We may, for example, be able to ascertain astrologically quite quickly that the reason that someone isn't moving forward is because he or she is still stuck in the grieving process from a loss that happened many years ago. Or we can perhaps see via the chart that a person's physical symptoms are reflective of long-term buried anger towards a parent or partner. Obviously bringing these hidden factors to light and talking them through can help enormously, but using a homoeopathic or flower essence remedy specifically designed to help and support a person through such a state can speed up the healing process.

Many therapies can help facilitate change, and a good practitioner will guide you in the direction you need to go in as well as offering emotional support. However, to think that any one therapy will cure you in the absence of making changes is a mistake. Many therapists are aware that treatment on its own, though often initially successful, is usually not enough, and if we don't change our lifestyle, thought patterns, emotional reactions or life path, the condition will recur a few months down the line. With this is mind, the therapies we use should be viewed as support and gentle nudges in the right direction.

Many astrologers become stuck with a client once the underlying reasons for a condition have been established. They know why people are the way they are but are unsure of how to help them shift. It is often useful for such astrologers to learn and use one of the therapies listed below or to work with a practitioner of such a therapy to gain greater results. The therapies are the ones that I feel work in harmony with astrology because of their links with the planets or with personality types.

Homoeopathy

Homoeopathy is perhaps the perfect therapy for use in conjunction with astrology as it works on an energy level and is based on personality types. The remedies can quite clearly be seen to form links with the signs and planets. Staphysagria, for example, is very Plutonic or Scorpio-like in its make up, being prone to deeply suppressed emotions, especially anger and hurt, and also relates to the sexual organs. The remedy mercury, not surprisingly, is for people mercurial in temperament, whereas pulsatilla accords with Pisces, Cancer or Libra types, being very gentle but clingy and sensitive. Homoeopathy, like astrology, also takes the whole person into account and remedies are frequently prescribed for the personality type rather than for the illness or symptoms.

Aromatherapy

The use of oils in conjunction with the signs and planets is something that is increasing. Although not quite as complex as homoeopathy, each aromatherapy oil does have a 'personality' and can therefore be used to help create balance and harmony. If you want to use aromatherapy in conjunction with astrology, try making a blend for your Sun, Moon and Ascendant signs. This is a simple, quick and easy way to help bring you back into your centre, and Patricia Davies's book *Astrological Aromatherapy* is a wonderful guide for people wishing to learn how to combine these two healing methods.

You can become qualified in aromatherapy within a year but, since so many people use oils in their homes, there's no reason why you can't use oils for yourself or, if you practise astrology, you can have fun making up blends for your friends or clients based on their chart.

Crystals

Crystals and gemstones are also tools that can be used with astrology as they correlate with the planets. For example, jasper, amber, topaz, citrine and quartz are stones of the Sun, so someone who is having a Saturn transit to their Sun may choose to carry one of these crystals close to his or her body for strength and support.

The chances are that your favourite stone correlates with the planet ruling your Sun, Moon or rising sign.

Herbs and nutrition

Nicolas Culpeper, the famous astrological herbalist, was and still is the leading authority on using herbs with the planets. Herbs are an ideal form of medicine to use with astrology as each planet and sign rules several herbs. Although a gross simplification of a complex subject, we would generally use the herbs ruled by the signs and planets that are weak in the chart – either by transit or natally.

Bach flowers

These 38 gentle flower remedies are similar to aromatherapy oils and homoeopathic remedies in that they address the patient's psychological and emotional type, which can be used to help with inherent difficult personality traits, as well as any emotional or psychological issues brought up by stressful planetary transits. The essences were developed by Doctor Edward Bach, who discovered that when the petals of certain wild flowers are distilled in water and left in the sunshine they can impart healing qualities. They work on the vibrational level balancing out the emotions so that a potential illness is healed before it manifests on the physical level. Plants, animals and children respond well to these remedies.

Australian bush flowers

Working on the same principle as the Bach flowers, but at the spiritual level as well as the emotional, the Australian bush flower essences are ideal for people who need more than a remedy to balance their emotions. They are ideal for dissolving blockages and painful issues, from a lack of abundance to sexual abuse. They are also suitable for healing past life issues, or for people needing auric protection – especially valuable for therapists, healers and counsellors. Because of their specific nature and wide range of applications from the spiritual to the emotional, Australian bush flowers are a good supportive tool to use in conjunction with astrology.

The subconscious therapies – journal, art and music therapy

Although these aren't therapies that link in with astrology in the same way as the therapies listed above do, they do work well with astrology because they tap into the subconscious and facilitate the release of long-suppressed emotions. Keeping a daily journal, especially during times of confusion or depression, is a wonderful way of discovering who you really are and what you really want. The idea is to write three pages of A4 every day at the same time and just see what comes out. You may start writing about your day, or what you're feeling. Or, if you're a complete blank, just write any old nonsense, or the same sentence over and over – even 'I'm a blank, I'm a blank, I'm a blank' – until eventually your logical left brain will get tired and make way for the spontaneous freeflowing action of the right brain. Prepare to experience feelings you didn't know were there, but also prepare to produce ideas, desires and insights into your daily life, vocation and relationships.

142

Art and music therapy are also valuable in the release of suppressed emotions and the expression of your true self. Many therapists incorporate art as a way of allowing their clients to express their feelings and it actually helps if you can't draw, since art therapy is about bringing colour to your feelings, not creating a technical masterpiece. Playing or listening to music can also provide a release for buried emotions. If you don't have any instruments then sing along to songs that express how you're feeling – the cheapest, quickest and easiest way to vent your feelings.

Counselling, psychotherapy and dream analysis

Counselling and psychotherapy are other therapies of the mind that work extremely well with astrology, as the chart points the counsellor or psychotherapist in the right direction. This gives them an understanding of the patient that would perhaps have taken weeks or months to get to through conventional analysis. It is my belief that all astrologers (and this goes for tarot readers too) should have some form of counselling skills, for reasons which should be obvious to anyone in an advice-giving role.

Dreams can provide fascinating insights into the unconscious mechanisms. Having an understanding of the language of dreams can help us understand our hidden motivations, desires and blockages, and for this reason it's well worth keeping a diary to record your dreams so that you can see any patterns and become more familiar with dream symbolism.

Matching therapies to personalities

In my years working as an astrologer and studying various therapies, I have come to the conclusion that no one therapy works for all the people all the time. So much, of course, depends on the nature of the issue and the personality of the client, and this is perhaps where astrology can be invaluable in discovering which therapies are ideally suited to which person. For example, suggesting a selection of intangible spiritual-based therapies for a strongly earthy person who needs to be able to see or feel what's going on may not be a good idea. Such a person would benefit from something more hands-on like massage or the Alexander technique, whereas a deeply airy person would enjoy the ethereal nature of therapies of the mind or soul like aura soma, homoeopathy and chakra balancing. Likewise, a more watery or emotional individual would probably benefit from one of the gentle emotional therapies, such as Bach flowers remedies, or counselling where they could discuss their feelings. Fiery people, on the other hand, would probably enjoy the inspirational active therapies such as art, music or drama therapy, or any method that gets fast results.

Which to choose?

If you are a practitioner, it's as well to have a little knowledge of the different therapies now available so you can point your client in the right direction if need be. Alternatively, you may be looking for a therapy for your own needs. Either way, with the staggering number of therapies now available, from the well-known ones such as homoeopathy, acupuncture and aromatherapy to the new ones such as the Bowen technique and aura soma, we may be forgiven for becoming confused when deciding which alternative path of treatment to pursue.

Never dismiss the power of intuition as it is quite often the therapies that we are drawn to and that interest us that will work the best. If, however, you're new to the world of holistic medicine or aren't drawn to any one particular therapy, a good starting point is to identify whether your issue or condition is physical, emotional, psychological or spiritual in origin.

Healing mind, body and soul

Working with the theory that illness can manifest itself on any of the four levels of our being, we can easily assess which level you need to focus on and therefore which type of therapy will work best for you. Obviously, many therapies work on more than one level and it's important to keep in mind that even what appears to be a minor or temporary physical problem has its roots at a higher level. So what follows serves as a general guide.

The physical therapies

If your symptoms are mainly physical in nature – that is, acute, brought on by poor posture, bad diet, lack of exercise, fatigue, general day-to-day stress, accidents or injuries – the following therapies may be able to assist:

- acupuncture
- Alexander technique
- allergy testing
- aromatherapy massage
- ayurvedic medicine
- biochemic tissue salts
- deep body massage
- herbal medicine
- homoeopathy
- hydrotherapy
- inversion therapy
- jin shin jyutsu
- naturopathy
- nutrition
- osteopathy
- reflexology
- reiki
- skenar

The emotional therapies

If your symptoms are chronic and mainly emotional in origin – that is, created through various emotional states such as anger, guilt, fear, hurt, sadness or depression – the following therapies may be suitable:

○ art or music therapy

○ Bach flower remedies

○ counselling

○ gestalt counselling

○ hypnotherapy

○ inner child work

○ journal therapy

○ kinesiology

○ past life regression

○ rebirthing

○ reiki

○ transactional analysis

The psychological therapies

If your illness is operating at the psychological level through neurotic behaviour, phobias, nightmares, insomnia, paranoia, schizophrenia, compulsions, obsessions, an inability to understand yourself or your life patterns, frustration with your habits or personality, or an inability to let go of the past and move on, the following therapies may work well:

- affirmations
- astrology
- autogenic training
- Bach flower remedies
- cognitive or gestalt therapy
- colour therapy
- counselling
- dream analysis
- homoeopathy
- hypnotherapy
- life coaching
- metamorphic technique
- past life regression
- psychoanalysis
- psychosynthesis
- rebirthing
- the 12-step programme for addictions
- visualisation

The spiritual therapies

If you suspect your problems stem from an imbalance at the spiritual level and you suffer from a lack of purpose, a sense of disconnection, a 'what's the point' attitude, drifting, not being true to yourself, not knowing who you are, or a deep unhappiness, the following may be of benefit:

- art therapy
- astrology
- aura cleansing
- aura soma
- Australian bush flowers
- chakra balancing
- crystal healing
- feng shui
- journal therapy
- meditation
- music therapy
- shamanic journeying
- tai-chi
- tarot/spiritual cards
- visualisation
- yoga

The 10 keys to well-being

The creation of health and well-being can be as complex as we are and the health gurus will each have their own golden rule that they feel is paramount. A lot also depends on the expert's area of focus. Doctors, for example, will advocate physical procedures such as regular screening, a healthy diet and exercise, whereas a Buddhist monk would be more likely to focus on the spiritual level, suggesting cultivating a peaceful mind along with demonstrating love and compassion as the vital ingredients for good health. Since we now recognise that good health is a combination of nourishment on all the four levels, we perhaps need a new model for creating health and well-being. It seems to be that there are 10 vital ingredients for the creation of health and happiness and if we incorporate these into our daily lives we should manage to keep illness at bay.

What follows, then, are what appear to be the common sense rules for establishing and maintaining health and well-being, taking into account the physical, emotional, psychological and spiritual levels. They are as follows:

1 Eat well

Eating well may seem like the easiest thing in the world, but it is becoming more and more difficult with our increasing reliance on processed and packaged foods, many of which contain harmful chemical pesticides and additives. Choose organic whenever possible, especially meat which otherwise contains traces of the antibiotics and growth hormones routinely fed to the animals. Better still, omit red meat altogether – it is hard to digest, lingering for five days in the digestive tract, and is associated with cancer and heart disease.

2 Sleep well

It is during sleep that our bodies are most able to heal and regenerate themselves, therefore stinting on sleep doesn't just produce fatigue, it also depletes your immune system leaving you more prone to illness or being unable to shake off a current ailment.

3 Exercise

It was once thought that intense exercise several times a week was the most beneficial. Now, though, it has emerged that you don't have to work up a sweat to keep your body supple and energised. Becoming seriously out of breath puts a strain on your system and releases damaging free radicals (why else are professional athletes and sports-people plagued by injuries?). Much better to pursue a gentle form of exercise that tones and invigorates rather than shatters your body. Yoga, walking, gentle cycling, horse-riding, swimming and tai-chi are ideal forms of exercise.

4 Avoid physical damage

This is common sense but yet it's amazing how many of us repeatedly subject our bodies to abuse in one form or another. Physical damage constitutes anything that works against your body, such as smoking, drugs (including prescription drugs), alcohol, fat, salt, sugar, pesticides in food, microwave ovens, mobile phones and pollution. Obviously the society in which we now live makes it impossible to avoid many of the problems listed above, but we can make an effort to reduce our exposure to them.

5 Cultivate a peaceful mind

A peaceful mind equals a peaceful body. If our heads are full of negative, angry, critical, unloving thoughts, our bodies will reflect this. Negative thoughts not only poison our bodies, they also keep us locked in unhappiness. A need for constant drama and excitement so that your life is a living soap opera reveals an inner lack of some kind. When you have the kind of natural high that comes from living your purpose and being in tune with the universe, it will be a blessed relief to get off the emotional roller-coaster.

Although the change from stressed-out to blissed-out doesn't happen overnight, small steps will reap rewards quite quickly. Joining a meditation or yoga class or following the philosophies of Buddhism or Zen might be all you need to shine a new perspective on life.

Studies show that those who meditate, as well as being more peaceful and able to deal with life's daily stresses, also have stronger immune systems.

6 Reduce stress

Stress in one form or another is a major factor in the health problems we face today. Many forms of stress manifest as a result of our lifestyle choices. We feel we must be able to do it all – have a career and a family, be a good lover and a good parent – but in trying to do too much we compromise our health and inner peace. If you find yourself with no time to yourself it's time to prioritise.

There are some forms of stress, however, that we can do little about. Bereavement, divorce, moving house and other major life changes bring inevitable pressures and in these cases we would do well to choose a supportive therapy or remedy that helps maintain our balance until the stress is over.

7 Love

The big one. If you can manage only one from this list choose love as its power is an inoculation against disease in all its forms. Love is God's essence. It is the universal energy that creates and heals all things. It is the antidote to all forms of fear and hatred. To have love in your heart is the ultimate healer that washes away all pain.

To cultivate more love, appreciate the wonder and beauty of all living things. See the miracle in life, your own and your neighbour's. Love your parents, your children, your partner, your pets, your home, your friends, the trees, birds and flowers. Every living thing from the newborn child to the earthworm is an expression of God's love and as such should be treated with love and respect. And that includes you.

8 Learn to let go

If there's one factor that compromises our physical well-being, it's holding on to the past. Anger, resentment and bitterness stored over many years will eventually manifest themselves on a physical level through heart disease, arthritis or cancer. As within, so without. It is impossible to be emotionally poisoned and physically well at the same time. When you look at it this way, the only person you are hurting is you. If you can't forget, at least learn to forgive so that you can move on and create a better future. When we consider that we create our own realties with the power of our thoughts, beliefs and actions, it becomes easier to accept our part in the scenario and learn from the experience instead of remaining trapped. Of course, cases such as child abuse are the sole responsibility of the perpetrator, but even then, as adults, we can look back and understand that these people were coming from their own place of pain. Such a philosophy is never an excuse for bad actions, but understanding a little bit why a person feels motivated or compelled to hurt others can release us from our own pain.

9 Self-esteem

It is difficult to maintain health and happiness if we don't much like ourselves. If you can't think of much good to say about yourself, ask yourself who gave you such a negative message. All babies are born as bundles of love. It is only later that we are taught to feel badly about ourselves, either through direct words or actions from our parents or other people, or through indirect actions such as death and divorce that children take personally.

Most of us have at least one area through which our lack of self-esteem is demonstrated – it could be relationships, money, career, friends or health. We can all, therefore, benefit from greater feelings of entitlement. Boost your self-esteem by focusing on your good points (if you don't know what they are ask your friends) and creating special time for yourself. A client of mine whose main issue was low self-esteem realised that she needed to make more time for herself so she could get to know who she really was. 'What I need,' she pronounced, 'is to have an affair – with myself!' She decided to cook herself nice meals instead of waiting for her boyfriend to do it, took herself on holiday and timetabled some quality 'me' time. Her self-worth is now no longer dependent on other people's reactions to her.

10 Purpose

To be devoid of purpose is to be drifting like a cork on the ocean. Each and every one of us possesses a unique set of talents, traits and abilities (as depicted in our chart) and as such we have a unique reason for being here. Deep in our soul we know this, which is why it is so demoralising and frustrating when we can't or don't know how to fulfil our reason for being. There's nothing worse than feeling like a square peg in a round hole because we are in effect being untrue to ourselves. Without purpose we may feel that our lives are meaningless, which leads to self-destructive behaviour and a subconscious death wish.

For some people their purpose is as obvious as the nose on their face, and they may realise it as early as in childhood. For the rest of us, it's a mysterious puzzle that takes many years to figure out. Our purpose usually involves many things – it's not just about our vocation, it is a summation of our entire being. Ultimately, the way to discover it is to just do what you're drawn to and not be put off by either your own fears or other people's protestations. Easier said than done, but a little courage can go a long way in directing us towards the destination that is our special place.

Of course, there are many other factors that go towards creating health and happiness. We could, for example, have included the importance of balance, creativity, fun and play, laughter, responsibility, wisdom, and altruism – the list is endless. But the ones that made it into the top 10 are, in my opinion, the most crucial factors when it comes to creating a happy, healthy and fulfilling life.

15

Case Studies

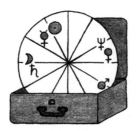

1: Charlotte

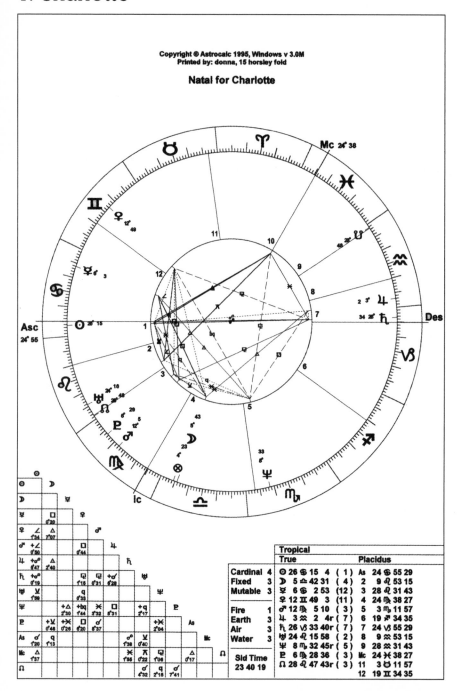

Copyright © Astrocalc 1995, Windows v 3.0M
Printed by: donna, 15 horsley fold

Natal for Charlotte

Charlotte was a very attractive woman in her early forties who came to see me with a variety of problems. At the root of most of them was a fear of failure and a huge lack of confidence and self-worth. Although she had obtained achievements in many areas, including a degree and competing for England at judo, she would always stop just short of success. The degree went unused and she suffered a back injury before obtaining her black belt in judo. Now she found herself studying counselling but was having doubts and reservations about completing the course, even though she enjoyed it and had received much positive feedback. The reason, she said, was fear of failing and not being good enough.

A single mother of three, she had been badly hurt by her ex-husband and as a result ensured that any subsequent men she saw didn't get too close. At the first sign of the relationship getting deeper she would find some excuse to end it. Consequently, she had little happiness in her personal life and was unsure as to her general direction and purpose in life. She had recently suffered two car accidents: in both cases a car had collided with her from behind – a universal sign to get moving if ever there was one! – causing her severe back pain.

Charlotte also wanted to learn how to be more playful and spontaneous, as most of the time she was a serious, overly responsible person. She wanted to be more relaxed and more able to play with her children. The issue of responsibility started early when her mother walked out when Charlotte was 10, and as the eldest she was left to take on a responsible role for her younger brothers and sisters.

This whole theme of responsibility and feelings of inadequacy can be seen via Saturn's position in Charlotte's chart – in Capricorn, opposite the Sun and Ascendant. This is akin to living in a straitjacket as Saturn urges us to be responsible, work hard and achieve. Saturn so pronounced creates a drive for material security, and outward success often masking insecurity. Note also that Saturn opposite the Sun is frequently linked to back trouble, as Saturn inhibits the Sun's natural tendency to stand proud and shine.

A majority of planets and her Ascendant in cardinal signs increases the need to achieve and be a success. Mars conjunct Pluto gives her an enormous amount of powerful energy which if not channelled constructively can backfire in the form of physical and emotional complaints.

During our first two sessions we discussed the importance of doing something simply for the love of doing it – because our heart resonates with it and not because we feel we ought. Such a philosophy can result in true success that doesn't revolve around acclaim and parental approval. We explored ways in which Charlotte could learn to relax and play more – the most important aspect she had to work on was that it was okay to make mistakes.

With the support of Bach flower remedies and her study of reiki, enormous improvements were seen very quickly. On the third session – coinciding with Jupiter crossing her Ascendant and conjuncting her Sun – Charlotte arrived a new woman. She was lighter, brighter, seemed much happier, and most importantly had booked a salsa holiday in Spain, which was a real opportunity to just let go and enjoy herself. She'd also just met a new man and with her newfound awareness of self-sabotage, she was much more enthusiastic and optimistic than when beginning her previous relationships.

2: Maddie

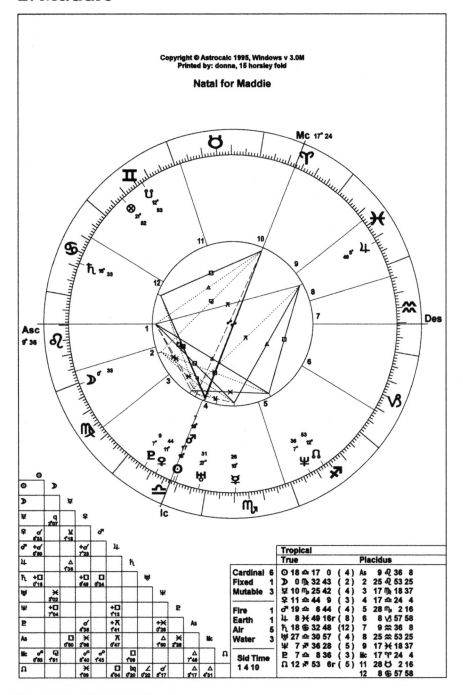

Copyright © Astrocalc 1995, Windows v 3.0M
Printed by: donna, 15 horsley fold

Natal for Maddie

		Tropical			
		True		Placidus	
Cardinal 6	☉ 18 ♎ 17 0 (4)	As 9 ♌ 36 8
Fixed 1	☽ 0 ♏ 32 43 (2)	2 25 ♌ 53 25
Mutable 3	☿ 10 ♏ 25 42 (4)	3 17 ♏ 18 37
	♀ 11 ♎ 44 9 (3)	4 17 ♎ 24 4
Fire 1	♂ 19 ♎ 6 44 (4)	5 28 ♏ 2 16
Earth 1	♃ 8 ♓ 49 16r (8)	6 8 ♑ 57 58
Air 5	♄ 18 ♋ 32 48 (12)	7 9 ♒ 36 8
Water 3	♅ 27 ♎ 30 57 (4)	8 25 ♒ 53 25
	♆ 7 ♐ 36 28 (5)	9 17 ♓ 18 37
	♇ 7 ♎ 8 36 (3)	Mc 17 ♈ 24 4
Sid Time	♌ 12 ♐ 53 6r (5)	11 28 ♉ 2 16
1 4 10		12 8 ♋ 57 58

157

Maddie arrived with various complaints. From the age of 16 she had had one health issue after another, from a lump in her breast to gynaecological problems, including polycystic ovaries. She was also diagnosed with candida and ME, thus leaving her feeling exhausted and very unwell for much of the time. Maddie had also suffered with back problems since having a nasty fall at work. She was becoming increasingly unhappy and frustrated in her work, and her symptoms were making her life miserable. She was prescribed a homoeopathic remedy to help bring her menstrual cycle into a more regular pattern, which would also help with bringing fears and blocks to the surface. What became apparent very quickly was that Maddie craved attention and her illness was a way of allowing people to focus on her and for her to absolve responsibility and be taken care of. This, we realised, was due to her childhood associations of illness when she received special treatment. Normally she played second fiddle to her brother, who received all the attention, but when as a child she was ill, attention turned to her and she received more love and care.

What is apparent from Maddie's chart is that she needs to shine and radiate. Her Leo Ascendant craves a certain amount of the limelight and the cluster of planets in the 3rd house denotes a need for self-expression. Her Moon in the sign of Virgo, along with her Leo Ascendant, shows a strong need for control – perhaps too much, and being able to just let things be is one of the important lessons she needs to learn.

Perhaps the most troublesome area in her chart is the square aspect between her Sun and Saturn. As with Charlotte, the Saturn influence causes Maddie to focus on the negatives, creating a belief that life is hard as well as doubt as to her own abilities. Helping Maddie to change her negative beliefs and working on her childhood issues formed the basis of my work with her.

Maddie began to make substantial improvements once she realised that her need for attention and special treatment was colluding with her symptoms and keeping her from getting better. Her subsequent physical and emotional changes were remarkable. She is now living out much more of her chart in the sense that she radiates warmth, energy and enthusiasm and is able to work a five-day week as well as enjoying a busy social life – something that was impossible previously. She has a new job that she enjoys more than the previous one and, though she isn't yet in the ideal line of work, she is expressing her creativity by taking singing lessons and is working steadily towards the other goals in her life.

3: Anna

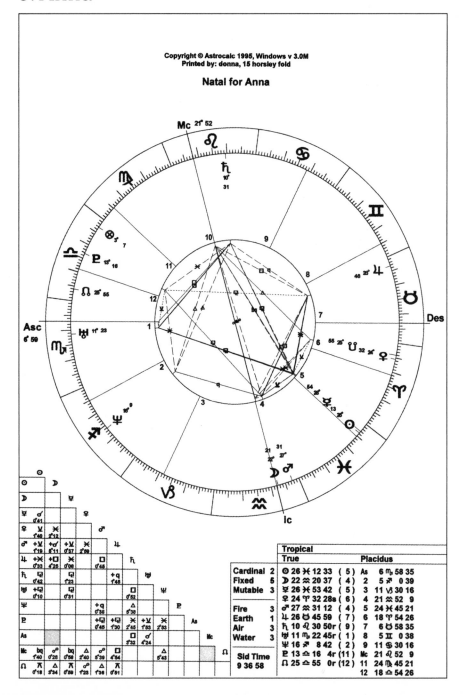

Copyright © Astrocalc 1995, Windows v 3.0M
Printed by: donna, 15 horsley fold

Natal for Anna

Anna presented me with a most interesting array of issues. It's fair to say that she was unhappy across the board. She was having a terrible relationship with her parents and sister, towards all of whom she felt a lot of anger. Her parents in particular she felt she couldn't relate to because they didn't understand her. She had no real friends but stayed within the social group she knew because she desperately wanted to be liked. Her relationship with her partner was becoming increasingly frustrating and she had serious financial problems. She had put her back out through sneezing and then shortly afterwards was the victim of a car accident (from behind) which made her back worse. Anna had also had a weak bladder that had been getting worse since the accident.

What became apparent very quickly was Anna's very low self-esteem and lack of identity, though this was masked by the forceful Scorpio Ascendant and Saturn at the top of her chart – both of which give the impression of being capable and in control. Underneath, though, was a very insecure and fearful girl. This lack of confidence then became the focal point of our sessions – if we could raise her self-esteem sufficiently, her life should begin to change. Almost immediately, there was success with her parents and sister: because she no longer demanded that they should understand her, much of the pressure was removed. For the first time they could talk without arguing and shortly after she spent a holiday with them.

We discussed ways in which Anna could resolve her money problems, which also involved her dropping her guilt at spending anything on herself (Neptune in the 2nd house) and she is now in the process of changing her life so that she can free up some money to dissolve her debts.

Her relationship with her partner, though, continues to cause her distress. She is desperate to move on and yet at the same time she is afraid of ending it for fear of being alone and of hurting her partner. Ending a relationship is also something she has never done before – she had always been the victim. Until she is able to do this, though, the bladder problems are likely to continue as they are connected to her need to let go of emotional patterns and a lack of clarity in her relationship.

Looking at Anna's chart, we can once again see the negative influence of Saturn bearing down upon her – the highest planet in her chart and square Uranus making her prone to accidents and back problems. Her Scorpio Ascendant makes it hard for her to let go and her Piscean desire to please and be a martyr is at odds with the strong Aquarius/Uranus influence to be an individual. However, as her self-esteem continues to rise, I am confident that she'll find the courage to leave the relationship and move on to build a happier life for herself.

16

Locating Your Planets and Aspects

This is a reference chapter to help you with the more technical aspects of understanding your natal chart. If you have a natal chart and a full interpretation, you will not need to go through this section, although you may find it useful for reference or as a place to jot down your basic chart details.

If you have a chart without an interpretation, you will be able to use this section to understand the symbols for the various planets and aspects so that you can extract all the relevant information and keep a note of it.

If you don't have a chart and want to work out your aspects from astronomical data, then you will be able to follow my step-by-step guide in order to understand the basics.

Astrological symbols

The zodiac signs

♈	Aries	♉	Taurus
♊	Gemini	♋	Cancer
♌	Leo	♍	Virgo
♎	Libra	♏	Scorpio
♐	Sagittarius	♑	Capricorn
♒	Aquarius	♓	Pisces

The planets

☉	Sun	☽	Moon
☿	Mercury	♀	Venus
♂	Mars	♃	Jupiter
♄	Saturn	♅	Uranus
♆	Neptune	♇	Pluto

The aspects

♂	Conjunction – together within 7 degrees
♂°	Opposition – 180 degrees
△	Trine – 120 degrees
□	Square – 90 degrees
✳	Sextile – 60 degrees
⊻	Semi-sextile – 30 degrees
⊼	Quincunx – 150 degrees

Step 1: Using the ephemeris

In order to work out your own planetary positions, you will need a copy of *Raphael's Astronomical Ephemeris* for the year of your birth. You can buy copies from the publisher (W. Foulsham & Co. Ltd: +44 (0) 1753 526769).

Turn to the spread for the month in which you were born and find the date in the left-hand column. Read across the columns to find the positions of the planets on that date. Starting with the Sun (☉), the data will show you which sign and what degree your Sun was in when you were born. For example, 15° ♋ 34' = 15 degrees and 34 minutes of Cancer.

There are 30 degrees in each sign, so if a planet is in 2 degrees of Taurus it has only just gone into that sign, whereas 29 degrees would indicate it's about to move into the next sign.

When you have identified the positions of your planets, record them on the worksheet below.

Planetary worksheet

My Sun is in	at	degrees
My Moon is in	at	degrees
My Mercury is in	at	degrees
My Venus is in	at	degrees
My Mars is in	at	degrees
My Jupiter is in	at	degrees
My Saturn is in	at	degrees
My Uranus is in	at	degrees
My Neptune is in	at	degrees
My Pluto is in	at	degrees

Step 2: Identifying your aspects

An aspect is formed between two planets when they fall within 7 degrees of each other.

In order to determine which of your planets form aspects, go down your worksheet list, starting with your Sun, and see if any of the other planets fall within 7 degrees either side of it. If they do, this means that this particular planet is forming an aspect with your Sun.

As an example, let's look at the planets for an imaginary client, Caroline, with a birth date of 6 July 1960.

- Sun is in Cancer at 14 degrees

- Moon is in Sagittarius at 4 degrees

- Mercury is in Cancer at 29 degrees

- Venus is in Cancer at 18 degrees

- Mars is in Taurus at 11 degrees

- Jupiter is in Sagittarius at 26 degrees

- Saturn is in Capricorn at 15 degrees

- Uranus is in Leo at 19 degrees

- Neptune is in Scorpio at 6 degrees

- Pluto is in Virgo at 4 degrees

In order to find out whether any of Caroline's planets aspect her Sun, we go down the list looking for planets that are within 7 degrees of her Sun. This would mean that, since her Sun is 14 degrees, we are looking for planets that fall anywhere between 7 degrees and 21 degrees.

We would then deduce that the following planets are aspecting her Sun:

- Venus (18)   - Mars (11)

- Saturn (15)   - Uranus (19)

You may be wondering what happens when a planet is at the end of a sign, as Caroline's Mercury is, at 29 degrees of Cancer. Again we would still look for planets within 7 degrees either side, so this would be from 22 degrees up to 6 degrees. The only planets that fall within these numbers are Jupiter (26 degrees) and Neptune (6 degrees).

We would then deduce that the following planets are aspecting her Mercury:

- Jupiter (26)

- Neptune (6)

Step 3: Identifying your hard and soft aspects

The next stage is to determine whether any of these aspects are worth looking at in health terms. The main hard aspects are the conjunction, square and opposition, while the main easy or soft aspects are the trine and the sextile. To save you doing the lengthy sums to work these out, simply check the grid opposite which shows whether your aspects are hard (H) or soft (S). Although the hard aspects are generally more significant, the soft aspects can relate to certain health conditions too, so check these out as well.

If the square is blank, this means that the aspect that your two planets form isn't one that we would normally consider, so you don't need to write it down.

Aspect grid

	PLANET ONE											
PLANET TWO	Aries	Taurus	Gemini	Cancer	Leo	Virgo	Libra	Scorpio	Sagittarius	Capricorn	Aquarius	Pisces
Aries	H		S	H	S		H		S	H	S	
Taurus		H		S	H	S		H		S	H	S
Gemini	S		H		S	H	S		H		S	H
Cancer	H	S		H		S	H	S		H		S
Leo	S	H	S		H		S	H	S		H	
Virgo		S	H	S		H		S	H	S		H
Libra	H		S	H	S		H		S	H	S	
Scorpio		H		S	H	S		H		S	H	S
Sagittarius	S		H		S	H	S		H		S	H
Capricorn	H	S		H		S	H	S		H		S
Aquarius	S	H	S		H		S	H	S		H	
Pisces		S	H	S		H		S	H	S		H

Key to the aspects: H = Hard   S = Soft

Continuing with Caroline as our example, her Sun in Cancer is aspecting her Saturn in Capricorn.

If we look at the grid we will see that Cancer and Capricorn aspects are represented by an H. Therefore Caroline's Sun is forming a hard aspect to her Saturn and she would then refer to the interpretation for the Sun aspecting Saturn, bearing in mind the stressful nature of the aspect. We would then see that the aspect from Venus to her Sun forms a hard aspect, while her Mars forms a soft aspect to her Sun. However, when we check Uranus in Leo against her Cancer Sun, we see that there is a blank space indicating that the aspect is a weak one and it is not necessary for her to consider this.

167

Although this is an easy way to work out which type of aspects you have, it has been generalised for ease of use. You will need to make adjustments when you have an aspect that is formed between a planet at the end of one sign and a planet at the beginning of another – as with Caroline's Mercury (29 degrees Cancer) and Neptune (6 degrees Scorpio). To ensure that the correct type of aspect is given, you will need to move the planet at the end of the sign into the following sign. For example, for Caroline's Mercury at the end of Cancer, read Leo. Looking at the grid for Leo and Scorpio, the aspect given is H for hard.

If any of your planets form aspects from the end of one sign and the beginning of the next, you will need to know the order of the signs. These always follow the same sequence, as in the chart, beginning with Aries (♈) and ending with Pisces (♓).

Caroline's aspects

Aspect 1	Sun hard aspect to Saturn
Aspect 2	Sun hard aspect to Venus
Aspect 3	Sun soft aspect to Mars
Aspect 4	Moon hard aspect to Pluto
Aspect 5	Mercury hard aspect to Neptune
Aspect 6	Venus hard aspect to Saturn
Aspect 7	Mars soft aspect to Saturn
Aspect 8	Mars hard aspect to Neptune
Aspect 9	Venus soft aspect to Mars
Aspect 10	Mars soft aspect to Pluto
Aspect 11	Uranus soft aspect to Jupiter
Aspect 12	Neptune soft aspect to Pluto

Your aspects

Record your significant aspects in the spaces below. You may not need to use all the lines.

Aspect 1	
Aspect 2	
Aspect 3	
Aspect 4	
Aspect 5	
Aspect 6	
Aspect 7	
Aspect 8	
Aspect 9	
Aspect 10	
Aspect 11	
Aspect 12	

Step 4: The interpretations

Congratulations! You've done all the hard work and identified your planetary aspects. Now you can turn to the relevant pages to read up on the interpretations. Remember to note that it is usually the hard aspects that cause the most stress health-wise, and the closer the degrees of your planets the more intense the aspect will be. For example, two planets that are within 1 degree of each other will be more powerful than two planets within 7 degrees.

Afterword

While we now have a dazzling array of alternative therapies, and conventional medicine continues to develop in its complexity, the stark truth is that we still have no cure-alls. Cancer, AIDS, heart disease, diabetes, arthritis, ME and many more diseases are running rampant with no prospect of a cure. Modern medicine offers us drugs and surgical methods that temporarily remove or suppress the condition, but they are really only delaying the inevitable. How many times have we come across people who, after having a cancerous growth removed, develop another one 12 months down the line? At the end of the day, responsibility for our own health lies in our own hands. We are the masters of our own destinies and if we took as much time trying to understand ourselves and our symptoms as we do running from one medical test to another, we'd be in much better shape.

When we realise that our bodies are constantly trying to heal themselves and that all we have to do is get out of the way and allow common sense to prevail, we can look forward to a healthier future.

Glossary

AFFLICTION: An affliction refers to a planet that is badly aspected by another – i.e. square or opposition.

AIR SIGNS: Gemini, Libra and Aquarius. *See also* Triplicity.

ASCENDANT: Also known as the rising sign. The sign of the zodiac rising over the eastern horizon at the time of birth.

ASPECT: An aspect occurs when two planets form a mathematical angle to each other – this can have either a positive or a negative affect.

BIRTH CHART: *See* Natal Chart.

CARDINAL: One of the quadruplicities. The cardinal signs are the four signs that share the same basic qualities of strength and determination – Aries, Cancer, Libra, Capricorn.

CONJUNCTION: This is an aspect that occurs when two or more planets are within 7 degrees of each other.

CUSP: This refers to an overlap between two signs or houses. It is said that someone born on the cusp of two signs will inherit some characteristics of the cusp sign. Whether this is the case is still debatable, with astrologers falling into two camps – those who believe in the cusps, and those who don't.

DECAN: Each sign is divided into groups of three – each of 10 degrees. These groups are known as decans – the first decan being born within the first 10 degrees of the sign, the second between the 11th and 20th degrees, and the third in the last 10 degrees.

DEGREE: The mathematical term used to pinpoint the exact position of signs and planets. There are 30 degrees in each sign.

EARTH SIGNS: Taurus, Virgo and Capricorn. *See also* Triplicity.

ELEMENT: *See* Triplicity.

EPHEMERIS: Tables of astrological information, listing the positions of the planets from time past to time in the future. This is how astrologers are able to predict the future and assess the past.

ESOTERIC ASTROLOGY: The study of the secret and spiritual meaning behind the signs and planets.

FIRE SIGNS: Aries, Leo and Sagittarius. *See also* Triplicity.

FIXED: One of the quadruplicities, the signs ruled by it are Taurus, Leo, Scorpio and Aquarius. These signs are the opposite of the mutable ones in that they are fixed in opinion and opposed to change and uncertainty.

FEMININE SIGNS: Taurus, Cancer, Virgo, Scorpio, Capricorn and Pisces are regarded as the feminine signs and have a negative polarity. They are likely to be more introverted and lacking in confidence than the positive masculine signs.

GRAND CROSS: Four planets forming a square in a birth chart – each being at an angle of 90 degrees.

GRAND TRINE: Three planets forming a triangle in a birth chart – each being at an angle of 120 degrees.

HARD ASPECT: *See* Affliction.

HOUSES: A house is a segment of the birth chart that corresponds with a certain area of life, and any planet in a house shows the reaction and level of importance that the subject places in this area of life.

IC OR IMUM COELI: The meridian point opposite the MC (q.v.). It occurs at the bottom of the chart and generally refers to the subject's roots and values.

MASCULINE SIGNS: Aries, Gemini, Leo, Libra, Sagittarius and Aquarius are regarded as the masculine signs and have a positive polarity. They are by nature enthusiastic, positive and more extrovert than the feminine signs.

MC OR MEDIUM COELI: Also known as the midheaven. Usually (though not always) occurs at the top of the chart in the 10th house and denotes the career inclinations and aspirations of the subject.

MERIDIAN: Point from which longitude is measured, e.g. Greenwich.

MIDPOINT: The middle point where two signs or planets meet, e.g. the midpoint of Aries and Gemini would be Taurus.

MUTABLE: This is the quadruplicity that the signs Gemini, Virgo, Sagittarius and Pisces share. This quality implies adaptability and a fluid, changeable nature.

NATAL CHART: The map of the soul or diagram showing the position of the planets at the subject's time of birth. An experienced astrologer can interpret this esoteric code and help the individual reach a better understanding of him or herself.

OPPOSITION: This is an aspect that occurs when two signs or planets are opposite each other.

POLARITY: Each sign has its opposite, and at times borrows from it. The polarities are: Aries/Libra, Taurus/Scorpio, Gemini/Sagittarius, Cancer/Capricorn and Virgo/Pisces.

PREDICTION: The method of astrology that uses the knowledge of the planets to predict the future.

QUADRUPLICITY OR QUALITY: The 12 signs are divided into groups of three and assigned a quadruplicity – cardinal, fixed or mutable.

RETROGRADE: When a planet appears to be travelling backwards from the earth it is said to be retrograde.

RISING SIGN: *See* Ascendant.

SOFT ASPECT: An aspect that is easy or harmonious.

SQUARE: An aspect that occurs when two signs or planets are 90 degrees from each other.

TRINE: An aspect that occurs when two signs or planets are 120 degrees from each other.

TRIPLICITY: The signs are divided into three groups of the four elements – known as fire, earth, air and water.

T-SQUARE: This is an aspect that occurs when two planets are in opposition and are squared by a third, forming a T-shape.

WATER SIGNS: Cancer, Scorpio and Pisces. *See also* Triplicity.

ZODIAC: The circle made by the Sun, divided into 12 sections.

Further Reading

Arroyo, Stephen, *Astrology, Karma and Transformation* (CRCS Publications)
This is a wonderful book focusing on spiritual and emotional growth. It looks at the karmic significance of the outer planets and includes chapters on relationships, Saturn and its cycles, transits and aspects. A real gem.

Cunningham, Donna, *Astrology and Vibrational Healing* (Cassandra Press)
A very readable and innovative look at astrology and health with a particular focus on how the planets Saturn, Uranus and Neptune can influence our health and how we can remedy their difficulties with the use of vibrational therapies.

Damian, Peter, *An Astrological Study of the Bach Flower Remedies* (Daniel)
Useful for astrologers who would like to understand the links between the flower remedies and the zodiac signs.

Davies, Patricia, *Astrological Aromatherapy* (Daniel)
The only book to help astrologers blend their art with oils and vice versa. Simple, easy to understand and nicely illustrated, a must for any astrologers interested in aromatherapy.

Dreyer, Ronnie Gale, *Healing Signs* (Doubleday)
A good book for finding out how your Sun sign affects your health. It includes tissue salts, aromatherapy oils and ayurvedic medicine to help balance the nature of your Sun sign.

Edwards, Gill, *Living Magically* (Piatkus)
You'll never look at the world in the same way after reading this. Gill has done a wonderful job of making metaphysics accessible to all in this fascinating study of how we create our own realities.

Hall, Judy, *Patterns of the Past* (Arkana)
A wonderfully deep and meandering exploration of how the birth chart can reveal karma and past-life issues. It also has a chapter on physical illness and how this can link to previous patterns.

Hay, Louise, *You Can Heal Your Life* (Eden Grove)
  Louise Hay made the body–mind connection accessible to all, but this book is so much more than a metaphysical health guide. Everyone should have a copy.

Jeffers, Susan, *Feel the Fear and Do It Anyway* (Arrow)
  A classic fear-busting book that will inspire you to move beyond your comfort zone and live life to the full. Wonderful if you're undergoing a Saturn transit.

Mayo, Jeff, *How to Read Raphael's Ephemeris* (W. Foulsham & Co. Ltd)
  A step-by-step guide to using an ephemeris to draw a birth chart, this will be useful if you decide to extend your astrological study.

Myss, Caroline & Shealy, Norman, *The Creation of Health* (Bantam)
  A serious study of how emotional disturbances can lead to illness and disease. The authors examine the whole process of health and illness and turn their profound insights towards many of the common health problems we face today, including cancer, heart disease and strokes.

Raphael's Astronomical Ephemeris of the Planets' Places
(W. Foulsham & Co. Ltd)
  This book of astronomical data is published annually and contains the positions of all the planets on every day of the given year. If you wish to compile your own birth chart, you will need a copy for the year of your birth. Individual copies are available direct from the publisher. Telephone +44 (0) 1753 526769.

Ridder-Patrick, Jane, *A Handbook of Medical Astrology* (Arkana)
  A traditional and very thorough examination of medical astrology. Includes diagnoses of your planetary aspects and how to draw up and interpret charts for your clients.

Shapiro, Debbie, *Your Body Speaks Your Mind* (Piatkus)
  One of the very best books for understanding how symptoms and illnesses are reflective of psychological and emotional issues. You'll never look at your body in the same way again!

Starck, Marcia, *Healing with Astrology* (The Crossing Press)
  A wonderful book packed with information on how to improve your health using your birth chart. It includes chapters on herbs, crystals, aromatherapy, music and colour and flower remedies.

Useful Addresses

The Astrological Association

The annual subscription to the Astrological Association of £31 entitles you to a bi-monthly journal that keeps you informed of the latest news and developments within astrology, plus articles, book reviews, forecasting techniques etc. There are also medical newsletters, conferences, workshops and seminars, so it is well worth joining.

Contact:
Kate Czerny
The Astrological Association
Unit 168, Lee Valley Technopark
Tottenham Hale
London N17 9LN
Tel: +44 (0) 20 8880 4848
email: astrological.association@zetnet.co.uk

The Wessex Astrologer

The leading publishers of a variety of astrological material, ranging from books and magazines (including the only magazine for serious astrologers – *The Mountain Astrologer*) to CDs and games.

Contact:
The Wessex Astrologer Ltd
PO BOX 2751
Bournemouth
BH6 3ZJ
Tel: +44 (0) 1202 424695
web: www.wessexastrologer.com
email: WessexAstrologer@mcmail.com

The British Astrological & Psychic Society

For courses and workshops in the divinatory arts.
Tel: +44 (0) 906 4700827
web: www.baps.ws
email: info@baps.ws

Scorpio Rising Astrology Services

Offers a range of charts, including your own personal health guide based on the information in this book, as well as one-to-one consultations – postal or in person. The School of Scorpio Rising offers a correspondence diploma course ideal for beginners.
Contact:
Donna Taylor
15 Horsley Fold
Clifton
Brighouse
West Yorkshire HD6 4HR
Tel: +44 (0) 1484 400872
web: www.scorpio-rising.co.uk
email donna@scorpiorising.freeserve.co.uk

Web sites

For free chart print outs:
www.astro.com

Bibliography

Cunningham, Donna, *Astrology and Vibrational Healing* (Cassandra Press, 1988)

Davies, Patricia, *Astrological Aromatherapy* (Daniel, 2002)

Myss, Caroline & Shealy, Norman, *The Creation of Health* (Bantam, 1999)

Ridder-Patrick, Jane, *A Handbook of Medical* Astrology (Arkana, 1990)

Shapiro, Debbie, *Your Body Speaks Your Mind* (Piatkus, 1996)

Starck, Marcia, *Healing with Astrology* (The Crossing Press, 1997)

Index

Old Moore's Personal Horoscope

Based on the Old Moore's prediction system, which has proved to be uniquely successful and accurate for over 300 years, these personal horoscopes offer an individual natal chart, character portrait and horoscope forecast for the next 12 months.

Copy and fill in this page or write all the details clearly in block capitals and send to:

> BJA
> PO Box 1321
> Slough PDO
> Berkshire SL1 5YD
> United Kingdom

Enclose a cheque for: £17 (from the UK)
$29.95 (from the USA)
£19 (from other countries)

Please make cheques payable to BJA.

Name: ....

Address: ....

....

Postcode: ....

Date, month and year of birth: ....

Time of birth (if known): ....

Place of birth: ....

Please allow 28 days for delivery.

☐ If you prefer not to receive mailings from companies other than those connected to Old Moore, please tick the box.